Law Enforcement's Role in U.S. Protection Against Agro-Terrorism

Copyright Page

TITLE: Law Enforcement's Role in U.S. Protection Against Agro-Terrorism

1ST Edition

Table of Contents

Law Enforcement's Role in U.S. Protection Against Agro-Terrorism

By Roberto Miguel Rodriguez

Chapter 1: Introduction to Agro-Terrorism and Law Enforcement's Role

Understanding Agro-Terrorism

Agro-terrorism refers to the deliberate use of biological agents or other harmful substances to disrupt or destroy agricultural resources, food supplies, or the economy as a whole. This subchapter aims to provide law enforcement professionals with a comprehensive understanding of agro-terrorism and its implications for national security. By understanding the nature of this threat, law enforcement can play a pivotal role in protecting the United States against agro-terrorism.

The chapter begins by exploring the concept of agro-terrorism and its potential consequences. It highlights the vulnerability of the U.S. agricultural sector, which not only contributes significantly to the economy but also plays a crucial role in ensuring food security for the nation. By disrupting the food supply chain or causing outbreaks of diseases in crops or livestock, agro-terrorism can have far-reaching consequences, impacting public health, economic stability, and social harmony.

To address this threat effectively, law enforcement professionals need to be well-versed in agricultural biosecurity measures. This subchapter delves into the various strategies and technologies available to safeguard agricultural resources and prevent potential attacks. It emphasizes the importance of surveillance and monitoring systems for early detection of suspicious activities and the need for robust crop protection technologies to mitigate the impact of potential threats.

Furthermore, the subchapter outlines the emergency response protocols that should be in place to effectively manage agro-terrorism incidents. It emphasizes the need for seamless coordination among law enforcement agencies, agricultural experts, and other stakeholders to ensure a rapid and effective response. It also highlights the importance of conducting comprehensive risk assessments to identify vulnerabilities and develop appropriate risk management strategies.

International collaborations in agro-terrorism prevention are also explored in this subchapter, acknowledging that agro-terrorism is a global threat that requires a collective effort to combat. It discusses the importance of sharing intelligence, best practices, and technological advancements with international partners to enhance prevention and response capabilities.

Lastly, the subchapter addresses the significance of public awareness and education in countering agro-terrorism threats. It emphasizes the need for law enforcement to engage with the public, agricultural communities, and relevant stakeholders to raise awareness, promote reporting of suspicious activities, and foster a sense of preparedness.

In conclusion, this subchapter provides law enforcement professionals with a comprehensive understanding of agro-terrorism and its implications for national security. By focusing on areas such as agricultural biosecurity measures, surveillance systems, emergency response protocols, risk assessment, international collaborations, public awareness, and advanced detection methods, law enforcement can play a vital role in protecting the United States against this significant threat.

Definition of Agro-Terrorism

Agro-terrorism refers to the intentional use of biological agents, toxins, or other harmful substances to target the agricultural sector with the aim of causing economic damage, disrupting food supplies, and instilling fear within the population. It is a form of terrorism that specifically targets crops, livestock, or any aspect of the food supply chain, with the ultimate goal of undermining the nation's food security.

In recent years, the threat of agro-terrorism has gained prominence due to increased concerns about national security and the vulnerabilities of the agricultural sector. Law enforcement agencies play a critical role in protecting the United States against agro-terrorism by identifying potential threats, implementing preventive measures, and responding swiftly and effectively in the event of an incident.

The agricultural biosecurity measures implemented by law enforcement agencies are designed to prevent, detect, and respond to agro-terrorism threats. These measures include enhancing physical security in agricultural facilities, implementing strict access controls, and conducting regular inspections to identify any signs of tampering or suspicious activities. Additionally, law enforcement agencies work closely with agricultural stakeholders to promote best practices in biosecurity and raise awareness about the importance of reporting any suspicious activities or potential threats.

The protection of the food supply chain is another crucial aspect in preventing agro-terrorism incidents. Law enforcement agencies collaborate with industry partners to ensure the integrity of the supply chain from farm to table. This involves implementing robust surveillance and monitoring systems to detect any potential threats or contamination, enhancing the security of transportation routes, and conducting thorough background checks on individuals involved in the food production and distribution processes.

Crop protection technologies and strategies play a vital role in mitigating the risks posed by agro-terrorism. Law enforcement agencies work alongside agricultural experts to develop and deploy advanced detection methods, such as sensor technologies and remote sensing, to identify any potential threats to crops. Moreover, they collaborate with research institutions to develop innovative strategies for crop protection, including the use of disease-resistant varieties and integrated pest management techniques.

In the event of an agro-terrorism incident, law enforcement agencies are responsible for implementing emergency response protocols to minimize the impact on the agricultural sector and ensure public safety. These protocols involve coordination with various stakeholders, such as emergency management agencies, agricultural organizations, and local communities, to swiftly contain the threat, mitigate damages, and restore normalcy to the affected areas.

Risk assessment and management are crucial components of agro-terrorism prevention. Law enforcement agencies conduct comprehensive assessments to identify vulnerabilities in agricultural infrastructure and develop strategies to mitigate potential risks. This involves analyzing the potential consequences of an agro-terrorism attack, identifying critical assets and vulnerabilities, and implementing appropriate protective measures to minimize the impact.

International collaborations play a vital role in preventing agro-terrorism incidents. Law enforcement agencies work closely with international partners to share information, intelligence, and best practices in agro-terrorism prevention. This collaboration includes joint training exercises, information sharing networks, and coordinated response mechanisms to address the global nature of the agro-terrorism threat.

Public awareness and education are essential in ensuring the proactive prevention of agro-terrorism. Law enforcement agencies engage in outreach programs to educate the public, agricultural stakeholders, and the broader law enforcement community about the risks and consequences of agro-terrorism. These awareness campaigns focus on promoting vigilance, reporting suspicious activities, and fostering a culture of preparedness within the agricultural sector.

Research and development of advanced detection methods are crucial in staying ahead of agro-terrorism threats. Law enforcement agencies collaborate with research institutions and private sector partners to develop cutting-edge technologies for detecting and identifying potential agro-terrorism agents. This includes the development of rapid diagnostic tools, early warning systems, and innovative surveillance techniques to enhance the nation's preparedness and response capabilities.

In conclusion, agro-terrorism poses a significant threat to the United States' agricultural sector and food security. Law enforcement agencies play a crucial role in preventing, detecting, and responding to these threats. Through the implementation of robust biosecurity measures, protection of the food supply chain, deployment of advanced detection technologies, and collaboration with international partners, law enforcement agencies strive to safeguard the nation's harvest and ensure the continued availability of safe and secure food for all.

Historical Overview of Agro-Terrorism Incidents

Introduction:

In this subchapter, we will delve into the historical overview of agro-terrorism incidents, providing law enforcement professionals and those interested in U.S. protection against agro-terrorism with valuable insights into the evolution and nature of these threats. By studying past incidents, we can better understand the challenges faced in securing America's harvest and develop effective strategies to mitigate future risks.

Early Incidents:

Agro-terrorism is not a modern phenomenon, as evidenced by historical incidents that date back to the early 20th century. One notable incident occurred in 1915 when German agents covertly introduced glanders, a highly contagious bacterial disease, into the United States horse population during World War I. This act aimed to disrupt the U.S. military and hinder its ability to mobilize forces.

Modern Incidents:

The 21st century has seen an increase in agro-terrorism incidents, highlighting the need for robust protection measures. In 2001, the United States experienced a significant attack on its food supply when letters containing anthrax spores were sent to media outlets and government officials. Although primarily targeting individuals, this incident raised concerns about the potential use of biological agents to contaminate the agricultural sector.

Another notable incident occurred in 2011, when an individual intentionally planted cyanide-laced apples in several supermarkets across the country. This incident highlighted the vulnerability of the food supply chain and the need for enhanced security measures to prevent such attacks.

Current Threat Landscape:

Agro-terrorism threats continue to evolve, necessitating a proactive approach to U.S. protection. The emergence of new technologies and strategies in crop protection, such as genetically modified organisms (GMOs) and precision agriculture, has introduced new vulnerabilities that could be exploited by terrorists.

Additionally, the interconnected nature of the global food supply chain presents challenges in terms of surveillance and monitoring. Ensuring the security of agricultural infrastructure and implementing effective emergency response protocols are crucial to minimizing the impact of potential agro-terrorism incidents.

International Collaborations and Research:

Given the transnational nature of agro-terrorism threats, international collaborations are essential in preventing and mitigating risks. Cooperation among nations enables the sharing of best practices, intelligence, and resources to strengthen agricultural biosecurity measures.

Furthermore, continued research and development of advanced detection methods for agro-terrorism are crucial. Investing in cutting-edge technologies and fostering innovation will enhance law enforcement's ability to detect and respond to potential threats effectively.

Conclusion:

Understanding the historical overview of agro-terrorism incidents provides valuable insights into the evolving nature of these threats. By studying past incidents, law enforcement professionals can better prepare for future challenges, develop effective prevention and response strategies, and work collaboratively to secure America's harvest. Additionally, public awareness and education on agro-terrorism threats are vital, as they empower individuals to recognize suspicious activities and report them promptly, further strengthening the nation's agricultural biosecurity measures.

Current Threat Landscape

In recent years, the threat of agro-terrorism has become an increasingly pressing concern for law enforcement agencies tasked with protecting the United States against this unique form of terrorism. The current threat landscape in agro-terrorism is characterized by a range of challenges that require the attention and cooperation of multiple stakeholders, including law enforcement, agricultural professionals, and government agencies.

One of the key elements of the current threat landscape is the evolving nature of agro-terrorism tactics and technologies. As terrorists become more sophisticated and innovative, they are constantly exploring new ways to disrupt and damage the agricultural sector. This includes the use of biological agents, such as plant pathogens or animal diseases, which can cause devastating consequences for the food supply chain and agricultural economy.

To effectively combat these threats, law enforcement agencies must stay up-to-date with the latest agricultural biosecurity measures. This involves implementing strict protocols and regulations to prevent the introduction and spread of diseases, as well as ensuring the protection of crops and livestock from intentional harm. Additionally, it requires the adoption of advanced crop protection technologies and strategies, such as genetically modified organisms or precision agriculture, to enhance the resilience of the agricultural sector.

Surveillance and monitoring systems play a crucial role in detecting and preventing agro-terrorism incidents. Law enforcement agencies must invest in sophisticated technologies, such as sensors, drones, and satellite imagery, to monitor agricultural areas and identify any suspicious activities or signs of disease outbreaks. This proactive approach allows for early intervention and containment measures, minimizing the potential impact of agro-terrorism.

Emergency response protocols for agro-terrorism incidents are another vital aspect of the current threat landscape. Law enforcement agencies must work closely with agricultural professionals and government agencies to develop comprehensive response plans that outline the roles and responsibilities of each stakeholder in the event of an agro-terrorism attack. These protocols should include strategies for rapid containment, decontamination, and recovery efforts to minimize the impact on public health and the economy.

Agro-terrorism risk assessment and management are crucial components of law enforcement's role in protecting the agricultural sector. By conducting thorough risk assessments, agencies can identify vulnerabilities, prioritize resources, and develop appropriate mitigation strategies. This includes the protection of critical agricultural infrastructure, such as storage facilities, transportation networks, and research laboratories, which are potential targets for agro-terrorism attacks.

International collaborations in agro-terrorism prevention are essential in today's interconnected world. Law enforcement agencies must foster partnerships with international counterparts to share intelligence, best practices, and resources. By working together, countries can enhance their collective ability to detect, prevent, and respond to agro-terrorism threats, ensuring the global security of the agricultural sector.

Public awareness and education on agro-terrorism threats are paramount in promoting a culture of vigilance and resilience. Law enforcement agencies should engage in public outreach initiatives to educate farmers, ranchers, agricultural workers, and the general public about the risks and signs of agro-terrorism. By empowering individuals with knowledge and awareness, they can act as an additional layer of defense against potential attacks.

Finally, research and development of advanced detection methods for agro-terrorism are crucial in staying ahead of evolving threats. Law enforcement agencies must invest in innovative technologies and support research efforts to develop rapid and accurate detection methods for biological agents. This includes the use of molecular diagnostics, biosensors, and data analytics to enhance the ability to identify and respond to potential agro-terrorism incidents.

In conclusion, the current threat landscape in agro-terrorism presents a complex and evolving challenge for law enforcement agencies. Through a multidisciplinary and collaborative approach, including the implementation of biosecurity measures, advanced surveillance systems, emergency response protocols, risk assessment, infrastructure protection, international collaborations, public awareness, and cutting-edge research, law enforcement can play a vital role in securing America's harvest against agro-terrorism.

Law Enforcement's Significance in Agro-Terrorism Prevention

Agro-terrorism, the deliberate use of biological agents to target the agricultural sector, poses a significant threat to the United States' food security and economy. As the primary guardians of public safety, law enforcement agencies play a crucial role in preventing and mitigating agro-terrorism incidents. This subchapter explores the significance of law enforcement in agro-terrorism prevention and highlights the various measures and strategies employed to safeguard the nation's agricultural sector.

One of the primary responsibilities of law enforcement in agro-terrorism prevention is the establishment and implementation of effective agricultural biosecurity measures. These measures encompass a range of actions, including securing agricultural facilities, implementing strict access controls, and developing protocols for handling and disposing of potentially hazardous materials. Law enforcement agencies must collaborate with agricultural stakeholders to ensure the adoption and adherence to these biosecurity measures throughout the food supply chain.

In addition to biosecurity measures, law enforcement agencies utilize various surveillance and monitoring systems to detect and deter potential agro-terrorism threats. Advanced technologies such as drones, sensors, and video surveillance are employed to enhance situational awareness and enable real-time response to suspicious activities. By leveraging these systems, law enforcement can identify and apprehend individuals involved in agro-terrorism activities before they can cause significant harm.

Furthermore, law enforcement agencies are responsible for developing and implementing emergency response protocols for agro-terrorism incidents. These protocols outline the coordinated actions of law enforcement, agricultural officials, and other relevant stakeholders to effectively respond to and mitigate the consequences of an agro-terrorism attack. Regular training exercises and drills are conducted to ensure preparedness and enhance interagency coordination in the face of such incidents.

To effectively address the evolving threat of agro-terrorism, law enforcement agencies must actively engage in risk assessment and management. By analyzing vulnerabilities and potential targets, law enforcement can allocate resources and develop targeted strategies to reduce the risk of agro-terrorism incidents. This proactive approach involves collaboration with agricultural experts, intelligence agencies, and other relevant entities to identify emerging threats and implement preventive measures.

International collaborations and information sharing are also crucial in agro-terrorism prevention. Law enforcement agencies must establish partnerships with their international counterparts to exchange intelligence, best practices, and technologies to detect and combat agro-terrorism threats collectively. These collaborations facilitate a more comprehensive understanding of the global agro-terrorism landscape and enable the development of effective countermeasures.

Furthermore, public awareness and education on agro-terrorism threats are essential in fostering a sense of responsibility and vigilance within the agricultural community and the general public. Law enforcement agencies must actively engage in outreach programs, workshops, and training sessions to disseminate information about agro-terrorism risks, preventive measures, and reporting mechanisms. By empowering individuals with knowledge, law enforcement can create a robust network of eyes and ears that can help identify and report suspicious activities.

Lastly, law enforcement plays a pivotal role in supporting research and development efforts to advance detection methods for agro-terrorism. By collaborating with scientists and experts in the field, law enforcement agencies can contribute to the development of innovative technologies and strategies for early detection and rapid response to agro-terrorism incidents.

In conclusion, law enforcement's significance in agro-terrorism prevention cannot be overstated. Through the implementation of biosecurity measures, surveillance and monitoring systems, emergency response protocols, risk assessment and management, international collaborations, public awareness and education, and research and development, law enforcement agencies contribute significantly to safeguarding the nation's agricultural sector against agro-terrorism threats.

Collaboration between Law Enforcement and Agricultural Agencies

In the fight against agro-terrorism, collaboration between law enforcement agencies and agricultural organizations is crucial. The convergence of their expertise and resources is essential to ensure the protection of America's harvest and mitigate the threat of agro-terrorism. This subchapter explores the various aspects of collaboration between these two entities and highlights their joint efforts in safeguarding the country's agricultural sector.

Law enforcement agencies and agricultural organizations must work hand in hand to enhance U.S. protection against agro-terrorism. By sharing intelligence and coordinating their activities, they can effectively identify potential threats and respond swiftly to any suspicious activities. This collaboration involves the exchange of information, joint training exercises, and the development of protocols to ensure a coordinated response in the event of an agro-terrorism incident.

Agricultural biosecurity measures play a vital role in preventing agro-terrorism. Collaborating with law enforcement allows agricultural agencies to leverage the expertise of law enforcement agencies in developing and implementing these measures. Together, they can establish robust systems to protect crops, livestock, and agricultural infrastructure from intentional harm.

Food supply chain security is another area where collaboration between law enforcement and agricultural agencies is vital. By working together, they can identify vulnerabilities in the food supply chain and implement measures to prevent contamination or tampering. This collaboration ensures the integrity of the food supply and safeguards public health.

The use of advanced crop protection technologies and strategies is essential in countering agro-terrorism. Law enforcement agencies can assist agricultural organizations in adopting and implementing these technologies. By collaborating, they can enhance the effectiveness of these strategies and stay one step ahead of potential threats.

Surveillance and monitoring systems are critical in detecting agro-terrorism activities. Law enforcement agencies possess expertise in surveillance techniques, while agricultural agencies have a deep understanding of the agricultural landscape. By pooling their resources, they can develop comprehensive surveillance and monitoring systems to identify and prevent agro-terrorism incidents.

Collaboration is also crucial in developing emergency response protocols for agro-terrorism incidents. Law enforcement agencies and agricultural organizations must work together to establish effective response strategies, including evacuation plans, communication protocols, and coordination with other emergency response entities. By collaborating, they can ensure a swift and coordinated response to mitigate the impact of agro-terrorism incidents.

Risk assessment and management are vital in agro-terrorism prevention. Collaboration between law enforcement and agricultural agencies can help in conducting comprehensive risk assessments and developing mitigation strategies. By sharing their expertise, they can identify vulnerabilities, implement preventive measures, and manage the risks associated with potential agro-terrorism threats.

International collaborations are essential in preventing agro-terrorism. By collaborating with international law enforcement agencies and agricultural organizations, American law enforcement can gain valuable insights and intelligence on global agro-terrorism trends. This collaboration facilitates the exchange of information, joint training initiatives, and the development of international protocols to enhance global agro-terrorism prevention efforts.

Public awareness and education on agro-terrorism threats are crucial in ensuring the vigilance of the general public. Law enforcement agencies and agricultural organizations can collaborate on public awareness campaigns to educate the public about the risks of agro-terrorism and encourage reporting of suspicious activities. This collaboration fosters a sense of shared responsibility and enhances public engagement in protecting the agricultural sector.

Finally, research and development of advanced detection methods for agro-terrorism require collaboration between law enforcement agencies and agricultural organizations. By pooling their resources, they can support research initiatives aimed at developing cutting-edge detection technologies. This collaboration ensures the continuous improvement of detection methods, enabling early detection and prevention of agro-terrorism incidents.

Collaboration between law enforcement and agricultural agencies is essential in securing America's harvest and protecting against agro-terrorism. By working together, they can leverage their respective expertise, resources, and knowledge to enhance U.S. protection against this evolving threat.

Law Enforcement's Role in Investigating Agro-Terrorism Cases

Introduction:

Agro-terrorism poses a significant threat to the security and stability of the United States, necessitating law enforcement's crucial role in investigating such cases. This subchapter will delve into the specific responsibilities and strategies that law enforcement agencies must adopt to counter this growing menace.

Understanding Agro-Terrorism:

Agro-terrorism refers to the deliberate act of targeting agricultural resources, including crops, livestock, or food supply chains, to cause harm, disrupt the economy, and instill fear among the population. Recognizing the potential devastating consequences, law enforcement agencies must prioritize their efforts to mitigate these threats.

Investigative Techniques:

To effectively investigate agro-terrorism cases, law enforcement must employ various techniques. This includes gathering intelligence through surveillance and monitoring systems specifically designed to detect suspicious activities within the agricultural sector. Leveraging advanced crop protection technologies and strategies, law enforcement can identify potential vulnerabilities and develop countermeasures to mitigate risks.

Collaborative Approach:

Addressing agro-terrorism requires collaboration among multiple stakeholders. Law enforcement agencies must establish close partnerships with agricultural experts, researchers, and international collaborators to exchange information, share best practices, and develop unified responses. By leveraging collective expertise, law enforcement can enhance their understanding of emerging threats and implement effective risk management strategies.

Emergency Response Protocols:

Preparedness is paramount in combating agro-terrorism incidents. Law enforcement agencies must develop comprehensive emergency response protocols tailored specifically to agro-terrorism threats. These protocols should include rapid mobilization of resources, coordination with relevant agencies, and effective communication strategies to minimize the impact of an attack and ensure a swift response.

Public Awareness and Education:

Law enforcement agencies play a pivotal role in educating the public about the threats posed by agro-terrorism. By disseminating information and raising awareness about the potential consequences, law enforcement can empower citizens to remain vigilant, report suspicious activities, and actively participate in safeguarding the agricultural sector.

Research and Development:

To stay ahead of evolving agro-terrorism tactics, law enforcement must invest in research and development of advanced detection methods. By collaborating with scientists and technologists, law enforcement can identify innovative technologies capable of identifying and preventing agro-terrorism incidents.

Conclusion:

Law enforcement's role in investigating agro-terrorism cases is critical for ensuring the security and stability of the United States. By adopting proactive measures such as surveillance and monitoring systems, emergency response protocols, and public education, law enforcement agencies can effectively combat agro-terrorism threats. Collaboration with agricultural experts, international partners, and investment in research and development will further strengthen law enforcement's ability to detect, prevent, and respond to agro-terrorism incidents.

Importance of Law Enforcement Training and Preparedness

Law enforcement plays a crucial role in ensuring the safety and security of the United States against agro-terrorism. With the increasing threat of intentional attacks on the agricultural sector, it is essential for law enforcement agencies to be well-prepared and adequately trained to tackle these challenges. This subchapter explores the importance of law enforcement training and preparedness in safeguarding the nation's food supply chain and agricultural infrastructure.

One of the key reasons for emphasizing law enforcement training is to equip officers with the knowledge and skills necessary to detect, prevent, and respond to agro-terrorism incidents effectively. By understanding the various agricultural biosecurity measures, crop protection technologies, and strategies, law enforcement personnel can recognize potential threats and implement preventive measures to mitigate risks. This training allows them to identify vulnerabilities in the food supply chain and agricultural infrastructure, ensuring early intervention and minimizing the impact of any potential attack.

Surveillance and monitoring systems are vital tools for law enforcement in detecting and monitoring agro-terrorism threats. Training enables officers to operate and utilize these systems effectively, ensuring that any suspicious activities are promptly identified and investigated. Additionally, law enforcement training should include emergency response protocols specific to agro-terrorism incidents. This ensures a coordinated and effective response, minimizing the spread of contamination and protecting public health.

Agro-terrorism risk assessment and management are critical components of law enforcement training. By understanding the potential risks and vulnerabilities in the agricultural sector, officers can develop proactive strategies to prevent attacks and enhance security measures. This involves collaborating with other agencies, such as agricultural experts, researchers, and international organizations, to share information and best practices in agro-terrorism prevention.

Public awareness and education on agro-terrorism threats are also essential. Law enforcement officers play a crucial role in educating the public about the potential risks and encouraging vigilance. By engaging with communities, conducting outreach programs, and participating in public events, law enforcement can raise awareness and empower individuals to report any suspicious activities.

Lastly, research and development of advanced detection methods for agro-terrorism are crucial for law enforcement preparedness. By staying at the forefront of technological advancements, officers can leverage innovative tools and techniques to identify and neutralize threats effectively.

In conclusion, law enforcement training and preparedness are vital in protecting against agro-terrorism. By equipping officers with the necessary knowledge, skills, and tools, law enforcement agencies can effectively detect, prevent, and respond to agro-terrorism incidents. Collaboration, public awareness, and continuous research are essential elements in ensuring the safety and security of the nation's food supply chain and agricultural infrastructure.

Chapter 2: U.S. Protection Against Agro-Terrorism

National Policies and Legislation for Agro-Terrorism Prevention

Introduction:

In the face of increasing threats to the nation's food supply chain, it is imperative for law enforcement agencies to be well-equipped with the knowledge and tools necessary to combat agro-terrorism. This subchapter explores the national policies and legislation that have been put in place to prevent and respond to agro-terrorism incidents, with a focus on the specific needs of law enforcement professionals. By understanding these policies and legislation, law enforcement can play a critical role in safeguarding America's harvest.

National Policies:

The United States has implemented several national policies to address agro-terrorism threats. One such policy is the National Bio and Agro-Defense Facility (NBAF) Act, which establishes the NBAF as a high-security research facility dedicated to studying and developing countermeasures against agro-terrorism. This policy provides law enforcement agencies with access to cutting-edge research and training opportunities to enhance their capabilities in agro-terrorism prevention.

Additionally, the Department of Homeland Security's National Infrastructure Protection Plan (NIPP) aims to strengthen the resilience of the nation's critical infrastructure, including agricultural facilities. Law enforcement agencies can collaborate with other stakeholders to develop risk assessments and emergency response protocols based on the NIPP, ensuring a coordinated and effective response to agro-terrorism incidents.

Legislation:

Several legislative measures have been enacted to support agro-terrorism prevention efforts. The Agricultural Bioterrorism Protection Act of 2002, for instance, criminalizes the act of knowingly possessing, using, or transferring a biological agent or toxin with the intent to use it as a weapon against agricultural interests. This legislation provides law enforcement agencies with the legal framework to prosecute individuals involved in agro-terrorism activities.

The Food Safety Modernization Act (FSMA) is another important legislation that enhances the security of the food supply chain. It requires food facilities to implement preventive measures to mitigate the risk of intentional contamination. Law enforcement agencies can collaborate with regulatory agencies to ensure compliance with FSMA requirements, as well as detect and respond to potential agro-terrorism threats.

Conclusion:

The national policies and legislation discussed in this subchapter provide law enforcement agencies with the necessary tools and guidance to effectively prevent and respond to agro-terrorism incidents. By understanding these policies and legislation, law enforcement professionals can collaborate with other stakeholders to conduct risk assessments, develop emergency response protocols, and enhance the security of the agricultural infrastructure. Furthermore, ongoing research and development efforts focused on advanced detection methods for agro-terrorism will enable law enforcement agencies to stay ahead of evolving threats. Through international collaborations and public awareness and education initiatives, law enforcement can play a pivotal role in ensuring the protection of America's harvest and the safety of its food supply chain.

The Homeland Security Act of 2002

The Homeland Security Act of 2002: Strengthening the U.S. Protection Against Agro-Terrorism

Introduction:

The Homeland Security Act of 2002 stands as a landmark legislation that revolutionized the approach to national security and protection against various threats, including agro-terrorism. This subchapter explores the key provisions of this act and its implications for law enforcement agencies involved in safeguarding the United States against agro-terrorism.

Enhancing Agricultural Biosecurity Measures:

The Homeland Security Act of 2002 emphasizes the need to strengthen agricultural biosecurity measures to mitigate the risks posed by agro-terrorism. Law enforcement agencies play a crucial role in implementing and enforcing these measures, ensuring the protection of the nation's food supply chain and overall agricultural infrastructure.

Utilizing Advanced Crop Protection Technologies and Strategies:

The act highlights the importance of adopting cutting-edge crop protection technologies and strategies to counter agro-terrorism threats. Law enforcement agencies must stay abreast of the latest advancements in this field, collaborating with agricultural experts to develop and implement effective countermeasures.

Surveillance and Monitoring Systems for Agro-Terrorism:

Law enforcement agencies are tasked with establishing comprehensive surveillance and monitoring systems to detect and prevent agro-terrorism incidents. The Homeland Security Act provides guidelines and resources to enhance the capabilities of these systems, ensuring early warning and timely response to potential threats.

Emergency Response Protocols for Agro-Terrorism Incidents:

In the event of an agro-terrorism incident, law enforcement agencies must be well-prepared to respond swiftly and effectively. The act emphasizes the development and implementation of robust emergency response protocols, enabling law enforcement to coordinate with other agencies and stakeholders to minimize the impact of such incidents.

Agro-Terrorism Risk Assessment and Management:

The Homeland Security Act underscores the significance of conducting thorough agro-terrorism risk assessments and implementing risk management strategies. Law enforcement agencies must collaborate with agricultural experts, researchers, and intelligence agencies to identify vulnerabilities, develop preventive measures, and respond to potential threats efficiently.

International Collaborations in Agro-Terrorism Prevention:

Given the global nature of agro-terrorism threats, the act encourages law enforcement agencies to foster international collaborations in prevention and response efforts. Sharing intelligence, best practices, and resources with partner nations enhances the collective ability to combat agro-terrorism effectively.

Public Awareness and Education:

The Homeland Security Act recognizes the importance of public awareness and education in mitigating agro-terrorism threats. Law enforcement agencies are responsible for disseminating information, organizing outreach programs, and educating the public about the risks posed by agro-terrorism, promoting a proactive approach towards prevention.

Research and Development of Advanced Detection Methods:

To stay ahead of evolving agro-terrorism techniques, law enforcement agencies must invest in research and development of advanced detection methods. The act emphasizes the need for collaboration between law enforcement and research institutions to identify innovative detection technologies and enhance their capabilities.

Conclusion:

The Homeland Security Act of 2002 has been instrumental in strengthening the protection of the United States against agro-terrorism. As key stakeholders in this endeavor, law enforcement agencies have a pivotal role to play in implementing the act's provisions, collaborating with various sectors, and remaining vigilant to safeguard the nation's agricultural sector and food supply chain.

The Agricultural Bioterrorism Protection Act of 2002

Title: The Agricultural Bioterrorism Protection Act of 2002: Safeguarding America's Food System

Introduction:

The Agricultural Bioterrorism Protection Act (ABPA) of 2002 was a significant legislative milestone aimed at fortifying the United States' protection against agro-terrorism. This subchapter delves into the key provisions of the ABPA and its significance in enhancing agricultural biosecurity measures, securing the food supply chain, implementing crop protection technologies, establishing surveillance systems, formulating emergency response protocols, conducting risk assessment and management, protecting agricultural infrastructure, fostering international collaborations, raising public awareness, and promoting research and development of advanced detection methods for agro-terrorism.

1. Enhancing Agricultural Biosecurity Measures:

The ABPA of 2002 revolutionized agricultural biosecurity by establishing stringent measures to prevent and respond to potential agro-terrorism threats. It strengthened the coordination between law enforcement agencies, intelligence organizations, and the agricultural community to mitigate vulnerabilities in the food system.

2. Securing the Food Supply Chain:

Recognizing the criticality of a secure food supply chain, the ABPA mandated the implementation of strict protocols to safeguard against potential agro-terrorism incidents. It emphasized the need for robust inspections, certifications, and traceability mechanisms to ensure the integrity of the entire food supply chain.

3. Implementing Crop Protection Technologies and Strategies:

The ABPA emphasized the deployment of advanced crop protection technologies and strategies to mitigate the risks posed by agro-terrorism. It encouraged research and development efforts to enhance crop resilience, develop disease-resistant varieties, and employ precision farming techniques to protect agricultural assets.

4. Surveillance and Monitoring Systems for Agro-Terrorism:

The ABPA called for the establishment of comprehensive surveillance and monitoring systems to detect and prevent agro-terrorism incidents. It emphasized the utilization of cutting-edge technologies such as unmanned aerial vehicles, remote sensing, and satellite imagery to enhance the efficiency of surveillance efforts.

5. Emergency Response Protocols for Agro-Terrorism Incidents:

To address the immediate aftermath of an agro-terrorism incident, the ABPA mandated the development of robust emergency response protocols. It emphasized the importance of coordinated response efforts involving law enforcement agencies, first responders, and the agricultural community to minimize the impact on public health and the economy.

6. Agro-Terrorism Risk Assessment and Management:

The ABPA promoted a proactive approach to agro-terrorism risk assessment and management. It encouraged the collaboration between federal, state, and local agencies to identify vulnerabilities, assess risks, and implement appropriate countermeasures to enhance agricultural security.

7. Agricultural Infrastructure Protection:

Recognizing the significance of protecting critical agricultural infrastructure, the ABPA allocated resources to safeguard key assets such as research laboratories, seed banks, and agricultural production facilities. It emphasized the need for robust physical security measures and the integration of cybersecurity protocols to prevent unauthorized access and potential disruptions.

8. International Collaborations in Agro-Terrorism Prevention:

The ABPA acknowledged the global nature of agro-terrorism threats and emphasized the importance of international collaborations. It facilitated information sharing, joint training exercises, and the establishment of partnerships with foreign counterparts to enhance the prevention, detection, and response capabilities against agro-terrorism.

9. Public Awareness and Education on Agro-Terrorism Threats:

The ABPA highlighted the significance of public awareness and education in countering agro-terrorism threats. It allocated resources to develop outreach programs, training initiatives, and public-private partnerships to ensure that citizens and stakeholders are informed about the risks, preventive measures, and response protocols associated with agro-terrorism.

10. Research and Development of Advanced Detection Methods for Agro-Terrorism:

The ABPA prioritized research and development efforts to advance detection methods for agro-terrorism. It promoted the collaboration between academia, research institutions, and private sector entities to identify innovative technologies that could detect and identify potential threats to the agricultural sector.

Conclusion:

The Agricultural Bioterrorism Protection Act of 2002 played a pivotal role in fortifying America's defenses against agro-terrorism. By enhancing agricultural biosecurity measures, securing the food supply chain, implementing advanced technologies, establishing surveillance systems, formulating emergency response protocols, conducting risk assessments, protecting infrastructure, fostering international collaborations, raising public awareness, and promoting research and development, the ABPA laid the foundation for a resilient and secure agricultural sector. Its impact continues to shape the efforts of law enforcement agencies and the agricultural community in protecting the nation's food system against agro-terrorism threats.

Other Relevant Laws and Regulations

In addition to specific laws and regulations pertaining to agro-terrorism prevention and response, there are other relevant laws and regulations that law enforcement agencies need to be aware of and comply with in their efforts to protect the United States against agro-terrorism. These laws and regulations provide a broader framework for ensuring the safety and security of the nation's agricultural sector and food supply chain.

One such law is the Federal Food, Drug, and Cosmetic Act (FD&C Act). Enforced by the Food and Drug Administration (FDA), this law regulates the safety and security of the nation's food supply. It establishes strict standards for food production, labeling, and distribution, and provides the FDA with the authority to take action against any food products that may pose a threat to public health.

Another important law is the Animal Health Protection Act (AHPA). Administered by the Department of Agriculture (USDA), this law aims to protect the health and well-being of animals in the United States. It establishes measures to prevent the introduction and spread of animal diseases, including those that could be used as weapons in an agro-terrorism attack.

The Plant Protection Act (PPA) is another key legislation that law enforcement agencies need to be familiar with. Administered by the USDA's Animal and Plant Health Inspection Service (APHIS), this law focuses on protecting the nation's plants and plant products from pests and diseases. It establishes regulations for the importation and movement of plants, as well as the detection and eradication of plant pests.

Additionally, the Homeland Security Act of 2002 is a crucial piece of legislation that law enforcement agencies should be well-versed in.

This act created the Department of Homeland Security (DHS) and consolidated various federal agencies involved in homeland security efforts. It provides the legal framework for coordinating and implementing measures to protect the United States against agro-terrorism, including the development of emergency response protocols and the establishment of surveillance and monitoring systems.

Law enforcement agencies should also be aware of international laws and regulations that govern agro-terrorism prevention and response. Collaborations with other countries are essential for sharing best practices, intelligence, and resources. International conventions, such as the International Plant Protection Convention (IPPC) and the World Organisation for Animal Health (OIE) guidelines, provide guidance on agricultural biosecurity measures and risk assessment and management.

It is crucial for law enforcement agencies to stay up-to-date with the latest advancements in crop protection technologies and strategies. Research and development efforts should focus on developing advanced detection methods for agro-terrorism. Public awareness and education initiatives should also be undertaken to inform the general public about agro-terrorism threats and encourage their participation in reporting any suspicious activities.

By understanding and complying with these laws and regulations, law enforcement agencies can play a vital role in securing America's harvest and protecting the nation against agro-terrorism. Their efforts, in collaboration with other stakeholders, are crucial to maintaining the integrity and safety of the agricultural sector and ensuring a resilient food supply chain for the United States.

Government Agencies and their Roles

In the battle against agro-terrorism, government agencies play a crucial role in ensuring the protection of America's agricultural sector. These agencies are responsible for implementing various measures and strategies to safeguard the nation's food supply chain, prevent potential threats, and respond effectively in case of agro-terrorism incidents. This subchapter will shed light on the key government agencies involved in the protection against agro-terrorism and their respective roles.

The first line of defense is the U.S. Department of Agriculture (USDA), which oversees agricultural biosecurity measures and coordinates efforts to enhance the resilience of the agricultural sector. The USDA conducts risk assessments and develops management strategies to mitigate agro-terrorism threats. Additionally, it collaborates with other agencies, both at the national and international levels, to share information and coordinate response efforts.

Another critical agency is the Department of Homeland Security (DHS), which has a specific focus on protecting the nation's critical infrastructure, including agricultural facilities and resources. DHS works closely with law enforcement agencies to develop surveillance and monitoring systems for agro-terrorism. It also plays a significant role in training and equipping law enforcement personnel with the necessary tools and skills to detect and respond to agro-terrorism incidents.

The Federal Bureau of Investigation (FBI) is another key agency involved in agro-terrorism prevention and response. The FBI conducts investigations into potential threats, gathers intelligence, and works closely with other agencies to ensure a coordinated response. It also plays a vital role in public awareness and education on agro-terrorism threats, disseminating information to law enforcement agencies and the general public.

Additionally, the Environmental Protection Agency (EPA) plays a role in agro-terrorism prevention by regulating the use of crop protection technologies and strategies. The EPA ensures that these technologies are safe and effective while also considering their potential misuse for malicious purposes.

International collaborations in agro-terrorism prevention are facilitated by agencies such as the Department of State and the Department of Defense. These agencies work with foreign governments and international organizations to share best practices, intelligence, and coordinate efforts to prevent agro-terrorism.

In conclusion, government agencies are at the forefront of protecting America's agricultural sector from agro-terrorism. Through their various roles, these agencies ensure the implementation of comprehensive strategies, surveillance systems, and emergency response protocols. Their collaboration, both domestically and internationally, is crucial in addressing the ever-evolving threats posed by agro-terrorism. Moreover, their efforts in public awareness, education, and research and development of advanced detection methods contribute to the overall preparedness and resilience of the nation against agro-terrorism.

Department of Homeland Security (DHS)

The Department of Homeland Security (DHS) plays a critical role in safeguarding the United States against a wide range of threats, including agro-terrorism. As law enforcement professionals focused on U.S. protection against agro-terrorism, it is essential to understand the role and responsibilities of DHS in this domain.

DHS is tasked with securing the nation's food supply chain and protecting agricultural infrastructure from acts of terrorism. They work closely with other federal agencies, state and local law enforcement, and the agricultural industry to develop and implement effective strategies to mitigate agro-terrorism risks.

One of the key areas of focus for DHS is agricultural biosecurity measures. These measures include implementing strict regulations and protocols to prevent the introduction and spread of pests and diseases that could harm crops and livestock. DHS provides guidance and support to law enforcement agencies in enforcing these measures and detecting any unauthorized activities that could pose a threat to agricultural biosecurity.

To enhance food supply chain security, DHS collaborates with various stakeholders, including farmers, transportation companies, and food processing facilities. They develop and implement security standards and best practices to ensure the integrity and safety of the food supply chain. Law enforcement agencies play a crucial role in monitoring and enforcing these security measures to prevent any potential agro-terrorism incidents.

DHS also focuses on developing and implementing advanced crop protection technologies and strategies. This includes researching and deploying innovative methods for early detection of biological threats, such as using remote sensing technologies, surveillance drones, and advanced monitoring systems. Law enforcement agencies should be aware of these technologies and work closely with DHS to effectively detect and respond to any agro-terrorism threats.

In the event of an agro-terrorism incident, DHS has established emergency response protocols to ensure a swift and coordinated response. Law enforcement agencies should be familiar with these protocols and be prepared to respond effectively in such situations.

DHS also plays a crucial role in agro-terrorism risk assessment and management. They conduct comprehensive risk assessments to identify vulnerabilities and develop strategies to mitigate these risks. Law enforcement agencies should actively participate in these assessments and collaborate with DHS to address any identified vulnerabilities in their jurisdictions.

International collaborations in agro-terrorism prevention are vital to ensure the security of the nation's agriculture sector. DHS works closely with international partners to share information, best practices, and intelligence on agro-terrorism threats. Law enforcement agencies should actively engage in these collaborations to stay updated on the latest global agro-terrorism trends and enhance their prevention efforts.

Public awareness and education on agro-terrorism threats are essential to ensure a vigilant and informed society. DHS conducts public awareness campaigns and provides educational resources to raise awareness about the potential risks of agro-terrorism and the role of law enforcement in preventing and responding to such incidents. Law enforcement agencies should actively participate in these initiatives and educate their communities about the importance of agro-terrorism prevention and reporting suspicious activities.

Finally, research and development of advanced detection methods for agro-terrorism are crucial to stay ahead of emerging threats. DHS invests in research and development initiatives to enhance detection capabilities and develop innovative technologies to counter agro-terrorism. Law enforcement agencies should actively engage in these research efforts and collaborate with DHS to leverage advanced detection methods in their operations.

In conclusion, the Department of Homeland Security plays a pivotal role in U.S. protection against agro-terrorism. Law enforcement professionals should familiarize themselves with DHS's responsibilities and collaborate closely with the agency to effectively prevent, detect, and respond to agro-terrorism threats. By working together, we can ensure the security and resilience of our nation's agriculture sector.

United States Department of Agriculture (USDA)

The United States Department of Agriculture (USDA) plays a crucial role in safeguarding the nation against agro-terrorism, ensuring the protection of our agricultural industry, food supply chain, and public health. As law enforcement professionals tasked with defending our country against agro-terrorism, it is essential to understand the USDA's role and the measures it undertakes to mitigate potential threats.

Agricultural biosecurity measures are at the forefront of the USDA's efforts. The department employs various strategies, including enhanced surveillance, risk assessment, and management programs to identify potential agro-terrorism threats. By monitoring the movement of animals, plants, and agricultural products, the USDA can detect and respond to any suspicious activities that may pose a risk to our agricultural infrastructure.

To ensure the security of our food supply chain, the USDA collaborates with federal, state, and local agencies, as well as industry stakeholders. These partnerships help establish effective surveillance and monitoring systems to detect and prevent agro-terrorism incidents. By leveraging advanced technologies and strategies, such as remote sensing, data analytics, and geospatial mapping, the USDA can swiftly respond to any potential threats and protect the integrity of our food supply.

In the event of an agro-terrorism incident, the USDA has established emergency response protocols to ensure a coordinated and effective response. These protocols involve close collaboration with law enforcement agencies, emergency management personnel, and other relevant stakeholders. By promptly mobilizing resources and implementing containment measures, the USDA can minimize the impact of agro-terrorism incidents on our agricultural industry and public health.

The USDA also focuses on international collaborations in agro-terrorism prevention. Given the global nature of the agricultural industry, it is crucial to work with international partners to share information, best practices, and technologies. Collaborative efforts help strengthen our collective ability to detect, prevent, and respond to agro-terrorism threats worldwide.

Moreover, the USDA recognizes the importance of public awareness and education in countering agro-terrorism. The department conducts outreach programs to educate farmers, ranchers, and the general public about the potential threats and the steps they can take to enhance agricultural biosecurity. By promoting awareness and providing guidance, the USDA empowers individuals and communities to be vigilant and proactive in protecting our agricultural resources.

Lastly, the USDA invests in research and development to advance detection methods for agro-terrorism. By continuously exploring innovative technologies, such as molecular diagnostics, sensor networks, and predictive modeling, the department aims to enhance our ability to identify and respond to emerging agro-terrorism threats.

In conclusion, the USDA plays a vital role in protecting the United States against agro-terrorism. Through its agricultural biosecurity measures, surveillance systems, emergency response protocols, international collaborations, public awareness campaigns, and research and development efforts, the USDA ensures the resilience of our agricultural industry and the security of our food supply chain. As law enforcement professionals, it is imperative to collaborate closely with the USDA and leverage their expertise to safeguard America's harvest and defend against agro-terrorism.

Federal Bureau of Investigation (FBI)

The Federal Bureau of Investigation (FBI) plays a crucial role in protecting the United States against agro-terrorism, a growing threat to the nation's food supply chain and agricultural biosecurity. This subchapter explores the FBI's efforts in addressing agro-terrorism and highlights their collaboration with law enforcement agencies and other stakeholders to ensure the safety and security of America's harvest.

As the principal investigative arm of the U.S. Department of Justice, the FBI is responsible for combating terrorism, including agro-terrorism, within the country. The agency recognizes the significant economic and public health consequences that could result from intentional attacks on the agricultural sector. To effectively counter agro-terrorism, the FBI engages in various activities, including risk assessment and management, research and development of advanced detection methods, and international collaborations.

One of the FBI's primary objectives is to enhance agricultural infrastructure protection, recognizing that critical agricultural facilities, such as food processing plants and distribution centers, are potential targets for agro-terrorist attacks. Through intelligence gathering, surveillance, and monitoring systems, the FBI identifies vulnerabilities in the food supply chain and implements strategies to mitigate risks. The agency also works closely with private sector partners to ensure the implementation of crop protection technologies and strategies that safeguard against agro-terrorism threats.

In the event of an agro-terrorism incident, the FBI is prepared to respond swiftly and effectively. The agency has developed comprehensive emergency response protocols to minimize the impact on public health and the economy. These protocols involve coordination with local, state, and federal law enforcement agencies, as well as public health and agricultural authorities.

To raise public awareness and educate law enforcement agencies on agro-terrorism threats, the FBI conducts training programs and workshops. These initiatives aim to equip law enforcement personnel with the necessary knowledge and skills to detect, prevent, and respond to agro-terrorism incidents. Additionally, the FBI actively engages in research and development to advance detection methods for agro-terrorism, focusing on innovative technologies that can identify biological, chemical, and radiological threats in agricultural settings.

Recognizing the global nature of agro-terrorism, the FBI collaborates with international partners to share intelligence, best practices, and resources. Through these collaborations, the agency strengthens global efforts to prevent and respond to agro-terrorism incidents.

In conclusion, the FBI is a vital component of U.S. protection against agro-terrorism. With its focus on risk assessment, infrastructure protection, emergency response protocols, and international collaborations, the agency plays a pivotal role in safeguarding America's agricultural sector. Through public awareness campaigns, research and development, and training programs, the FBI ensures that law enforcement agencies are well-prepared to address the evolving threats posed by agro-terrorism.

Chapter 3: Agricultural Biosecurity Measures

Biosecurity Importance in Agriculture

Biosecurity is of utmost importance in agriculture, especially in the context of protecting the United States against agro-terrorism. Agro-terrorism refers to deliberate acts aimed at causing harm to the agricultural industry, including crops, livestock, and the food supply chain. As law enforcement professionals, understanding the significance of biosecurity measures in agriculture is crucial to ensuring the protection of our nation's food supply and agricultural infrastructure.

Agricultural biosecurity measures play a vital role in preventing and mitigating the risks associated with agro-terrorism. These measures encompass a range of strategies aimed at safeguarding plants, animals, and the environment from potential threats. By implementing strict biosecurity protocols, law enforcement agencies can effectively prevent the introduction and spread of pests, diseases, and invasive species that could disrupt agricultural operations.

Additionally, the security of the food supply chain is a critical aspect of biosecurity in agriculture. Law enforcement plays a crucial role in ensuring the integrity and safety of the entire food supply chain, from farm to table. By collaborating with other stakeholders, such as farmers, processors, and distributors, law enforcement can help identify vulnerabilities and establish robust security measures to protect against agro-terrorism threats.

Crop protection technologies and strategies are essential components of biosecurity in agriculture. Law enforcement should stay updated on the latest advancements in crop protection, including innovative pest control methods, disease-resistant crop varieties, and precision agriculture techniques. By promoting the adoption of these technologies, law enforcement can enhance the resilience of the agricultural sector against potential agro-terrorism incidents.

Surveillance and monitoring systems are vital tools for detecting and responding to agro-terrorism threats. Law enforcement agencies should work closely with agricultural stakeholders to develop comprehensive surveillance programs that enable early detection of any suspicious activities or signs of disease outbreaks. Rapid and effective response protocols should also be established to minimize the impact of agro-terrorism incidents on the agricultural industry.

Agro-terrorism risk assessment and management are integral parts of biosecurity in agriculture. Law enforcement agencies should collaborate with agricultural experts and researchers to identify potential vulnerabilities and develop risk management strategies. By conducting thorough risk assessments, law enforcement can proactively address potential threats and allocate resources effectively.

Furthermore, protecting agricultural infrastructure is crucial to ensuring the continuity of food production. Law enforcement professionals should work closely with farmers and other stakeholders to enhance the security of critical infrastructure, such as irrigation systems, storage facilities, and transportation networks. By fortifying these assets, law enforcement can minimize the potential for agro-terrorism attacks and maintain the stability of the agricultural sector.

International collaborations in agro-terrorism prevention are essential for addressing the global nature of the threat. Law enforcement agencies should establish partnerships with international counterparts to share best practices, intelligence, and resources. By fostering these collaborations, law enforcement can enhance the effectiveness of agro-terrorism prevention efforts on a global scale.

Public awareness and education on agro-terrorism threats are key to fostering a vigilant and informed society. Law enforcement should engage in public outreach initiatives to raise awareness about agro-terrorism risks and encourage the reporting of suspicious activities. By educating the public, law enforcement can enlist the support of citizens in safeguarding the agricultural industry and protecting the nation's food supply.

Lastly, research and development of advanced detection methods are crucial for staying ahead of evolving agro-terrorism threats. Law enforcement agencies should support and collaborate with research institutions to develop innovative detection technologies that can identify potential threats rapidly and accurately. By investing in research and development, law enforcement can strengthen the nation's defense against agro-terrorism.

In conclusion, biosecurity is of paramount importance in agriculture, especially in the context of agro-terrorism prevention. Law enforcement professionals play a critical role in ensuring the protection of the United States against agro-terrorism by implementing and promoting biosecurity measures, collaborating with stakeholders, and staying updated on the latest advancements in crop protection and surveillance technologies. By focusing on agricultural infrastructure protection, international collaborations, public awareness, and research and development, law enforcement can effectively mitigate the risks associated with agro-terrorism and safeguard our nation's food supply.

Definition of Agricultural Biosecurity

Agricultural biosecurity refers to the set of measures and strategies implemented to safeguard the nation's agricultural and food supply chain from intentional acts of agro-terrorism or unintentional introduction of pests, diseases, or other biological threats. It encompasses a broad range of practices designed to prevent, detect, and respond to threats that could potentially devastate the agricultural sector and compromise food security.

In the context of U.S. protection against agro-terrorism, agricultural biosecurity plays a crucial role in maintaining the integrity and resilience of the nation's food system. Law enforcement agencies have a critical responsibility in collaborating with other stakeholders to ensure the effective implementation of agricultural biosecurity measures.

The primary objective of agricultural biosecurity is to prevent the intentional introduction of biological agents that could harm crops, livestock, or the environment. This involves implementing strict protocols and regulations to control the movement of people, animals, and goods across international borders, as well as within the country. By enhancing surveillance and monitoring systems, law enforcement agencies can identify and intercept potential threats at various points along the food supply chain.

Furthermore, agricultural biosecurity encompasses emergency response protocols to mitigate the impact of agro-terrorism incidents. Law enforcement agencies must be prepared to swiftly respond to any suspected or confirmed act of agro-terrorism, coordinating with relevant agencies to minimize the spread of biological threats and ensure the safety of agricultural assets.

Risk assessment and management are also critical components of agricultural biosecurity. By conducting thorough assessments of vulnerabilities and potential threats, law enforcement agencies can develop targeted strategies to mitigate risks. This may include enhancing agricultural infrastructure protection, investing in research and development of advanced detection methods, and fostering international collaborations to share knowledge, intelligence, and best practices.

Moreover, public awareness and education on agro-terrorism threats are vital in engaging communities and fostering a collective commitment to agricultural biosecurity. Law enforcement agencies can play a pivotal role in disseminating information, conducting training programs, and encouraging stakeholders to implement biosecurity measures.

In conclusion, agricultural biosecurity is essential to protect the nation's agricultural sector and ensure the security and safety of the food supply chain. Law enforcement agencies have a crucial role to play in implementing and enforcing biosecurity measures, collaborating with other stakeholders, and developing strategies to prevent, detect, and respond to agro-terrorism threats. By prioritizing agricultural biosecurity, law enforcement can contribute significantly to securing America's harvest and safeguarding national food security.

The Economic and Social Impacts of Agro-Terrorism

Agro-terrorism poses a significant threat not only to our national security but also to our economy and social fabric. This subchapter explores the economic and social impacts of agro-terrorism and highlights the essential role of law enforcement in protecting against this threat.

The U.S. economy heavily relies on agriculture, with the agricultural sector contributing significantly to the GDP and employing millions of people. An agro-terrorism attack could disrupt the entire food supply chain, leading to severe economic consequences. Such an attack could target crops, livestock, or agricultural infrastructure, causing massive financial losses for farmers, businesses, and the government. The resulting scarcity of food and rising prices would burden households and strain the already struggling economy.

Beyond the immediate economic fallout, agro-terrorism can have long-lasting social impacts. A disruption in the food supply chain could lead to food shortages, creating panic, civil unrest, and even social instability. The psychological effects on the population, particularly the vulnerable communities who rely heavily on affordable food, cannot be underestimated. Additionally, the loss of livelihoods in rural areas could lead to migration, straining urban resources and exacerbating social tensions.

To mitigate these risks, law enforcement plays a critical role in protecting against agro-terrorism. They are responsible for implementing and enforcing agricultural biosecurity measures, ensuring the security of the food supply chain, and safeguarding agricultural infrastructure. Through their surveillance and monitoring systems, law enforcement can identify potential threats and respond swiftly to prevent or mitigate an agro-terrorism incident. They are also instrumental in developing emergency response protocols, conducting risk assessments, and managing agro-terrorism incidents effectively.

International collaborations in agro-terrorism prevention are vital as well. Sharing intelligence, best practices, and resources with other countries can enhance our collective ability to prevent and respond to agro-terrorism threats. Law enforcement agencies must actively participate in these collaborations to stay ahead of evolving threats and ensure that our agricultural systems remain secure.

Public awareness and education on agro-terrorism threats are essential in mobilizing communities and increasing vigilance. Law enforcement agencies can partner with other stakeholders, such as agricultural organizations and educational institutions, to raise awareness about the potential consequences of agro-terrorism and educate the public on preventive measures. Additionally, research and development of advanced detection methods for agro-terrorism should be prioritized to enhance our ability to identify and intercept potential threats.

In conclusion, the economic and social impacts of agro-terrorism are far-reaching and require a comprehensive and coordinated response from law enforcement and other stakeholders. By understanding these impacts and taking proactive measures, we can protect our agricultural systems, maintain economic stability, and ensure the well-being of our society.

Biosecurity Practices for Farms and Agricultural Facilities

Introduction:

Biosecurity measures play a critical role in protecting farms and agricultural facilities from potential agro-terrorism threats. Law enforcement agencies have a vital role to play in ensuring the safety and security of the nation's food supply chain. This subchapter explores various biosecurity practices that can be implemented to safeguard farms and agricultural facilities against agro-terrorism incidents.

I. Importance of Agricultural Biosecurity Measures:

Agricultural biosecurity measures are crucial in preventing and mitigating the risks associated with agro-terrorism. These measures include implementing strict access control, maintaining secure perimeters, and establishing robust internal controls. Law enforcement agencies can collaborate with farm owners and operators to develop comprehensive biosecurity plans tailored to their unique needs.

II. Enhancing Food Supply Chain Security:

Protecting the food supply chain is paramount in preventing agro-terrorism incidents. Law enforcement agencies should work closely with farmers, transporters, and other stakeholders to ensure the secure transportation, storage, and distribution of agricultural products. This can be achieved through increased surveillance, monitoring systems, and the use of advanced technologies for early detection of any suspicious activities.

III. Crop Protection Technologies and Strategies:

Utilizing advanced technologies and implementing effective crop protection strategies are essential in safeguarding farms against agro-terrorism threats. Law enforcement agencies can collaborate with agricultural researchers and industry experts to develop and promote innovative solutions such as genetically modified crops, pest control methods, and precision agriculture techniques that enhance crop resilience and reduce vulnerabilities.

IV. Surveillance and Monitoring Systems for Agro-Terrorism:

Installing surveillance and monitoring systems is crucial to detect and deter potential agro-terrorism incidents. Law enforcement agencies can assist farms and agricultural facilities in implementing comprehensive surveillance programs, including the use of drones, cameras, and other monitoring technologies. Regular audits and inspections can ensure the integrity of these systems and identify any vulnerabilities that need to be addressed.

V. Emergency Response Protocols for Agro-Terrorism Incidents:

Developing robust emergency response protocols is vital to minimize the impact of agro-terrorism incidents. Law enforcement agencies should collaborate with farmers, emergency management agencies, and relevant stakeholders to establish clear protocols for reporting and responding to potential threats. Regular drills and exercises can help ensure a coordinated response in the event of an agro-terrorism incident.

VI. Agro-Terrorism Risk Assessment and Management:

Conducting thorough risk assessments is crucial in identifying and managing agro-terrorism risks. Law enforcement agencies can work with agricultural experts to assess vulnerabilities and develop mitigation strategies. These strategies may include physical security enhancements, employee training programs, and contingency plans for emergency situations.

VII. International Collaborations in Agro-Terrorism Prevention:

Agro-terrorism threats are not limited to national borders, necessitating international collaborations. Law enforcement agencies can work with their counterparts in other countries to share intelligence, best practices, and technologies to combat agro-terrorism. Joint training exercises and information-sharing platforms can enhance global efforts to prevent and respond to agro-terrorism incidents.

VIII. Public Awareness and Education on Agro-Terrorism Threats:

Raising public awareness about agro-terrorism threats is essential in fostering a proactive and vigilant society. Law enforcement agencies should develop public education campaigns to inform farmers, agricultural workers, and the general public about the potential risks and the importance of biosecurity measures. This can be achieved through workshops, seminars, and informational materials.

IX. Research and Development of Advanced Detection Methods for Agro-Terrorism:

Continued research and development of advanced detection methods are vital in staying ahead of emerging agro-terrorism threats. Law enforcement agencies can collaborate with scientific institutions, agricultural researchers, and technology companies to develop cutting-edge detection technologies. Funding and support for research initiatives are crucial to drive innovation in this field.

Conclusion:

Biosecurity practices are crucial in protecting farms and agricultural facilities from agro-terrorism threats. Law enforcement agencies have a critical role to play in collaborating with farmers, industry experts, and international partners to implement robust biosecurity measures, enhance surveillance and monitoring systems, develop emergency response protocols, and raise public awareness. By prioritizing agricultural biosecurity, we can ensure the safety and security of our nation's food supply chain.

Access Control and Perimeter Security

In the realm of U.S. protection against agro-terrorism, access control and perimeter security play a vital role in safeguarding our nation's agricultural resources and food supply chain. Law enforcement agencies have a critical responsibility in implementing and enforcing robust security measures to mitigate the risk of agro-terrorism incidents.

Access control refers to the practice of regulating entry and exit points to agricultural facilities, research centers, and other critical infrastructure. It involves employing various physical and technological measures to restrict unauthorized access and prevent potential acts of sabotage or contamination. Law enforcement agencies must collaborate with agricultural stakeholders to develop and implement effective access control protocols tailored to the unique characteristics of agricultural sites.

Perimeter security focuses on fortifying the boundaries of agricultural facilities to deter and detect potential threats. This encompasses the installation of fencing, barriers, and surveillance systems to create a physical deterrent and establish a clear boundary between public and restricted areas. Law enforcement plays a crucial role in conducting regular patrols, monitoring surveillance feeds, and responding promptly to any breaches or suspicious activities.

To enhance access control and perimeter security, law enforcement agencies should actively engage in the adoption of agricultural biosecurity measures. This involves implementing strict visitor management protocols, employee background checks, and credentialing systems to ensure that only authorized individuals can access sensitive areas. Additionally, the use of advanced biometric technologies, such as fingerprint or iris recognition, can further enhance security measures.

Surveillance and monitoring systems are essential components of access control and perimeter security. Law enforcement agencies should collaborate with agricultural stakeholders to deploy state-of-the-art surveillance technologies, such as CCTV cameras, motion sensors, and drones, to monitor agricultural facilities and quickly identify any potential threats or suspicious activities. These systems should be integrated with advanced analytics software to enable real-time monitoring and automated alerts to law enforcement personnel.

Emergency response protocols for agro-terrorism incidents should also be developed and implemented. Law enforcement agencies should work closely with agricultural stakeholders to establish comprehensive response plans that outline procedures for containment, decontamination, and investigation. Regular training and exercises should be conducted to ensure that law enforcement personnel are well-prepared to handle agro-terrorism incidents effectively.

Furthermore, law enforcement agencies must actively engage in agro-terrorism risk assessment and management. By conducting thorough assessments of vulnerabilities and potential threats, law enforcement can identify priority areas for security enhancements and allocate resources accordingly. This proactive approach allows for the development of targeted security strategies and the implementation of cost-effective measures.

International collaborations in agro-terrorism prevention are crucial in our interconnected world. Law enforcement agencies should foster partnerships with international counterparts to share best practices, intelligence, and expertise in combating agro-terrorism. Collaborative efforts can help identify emerging threats, enhance detection capabilities, and establish a unified response to agro-terrorism incidents.

Public awareness and education on agro-terrorism threats should be a priority for law enforcement agencies. By engaging with the public, agricultural stakeholders, and educational institutions, law enforcement can raise awareness about the potential consequences of agro-terrorism and encourage reporting of suspicious activities. This outreach effort can also facilitate partnerships with the community, improving information sharing and fostering a united front against agro-terrorism.

Finally, research and development of advanced detection methods for agro-terrorism should be supported by law enforcement agencies. By collaborating with academic institutions and industry experts, law enforcement can stay at the forefront of technology and innovation. This research can lead to the development of cutting-edge detection tools, such as rapid diagnostic tests, remote sensing technologies, and traceability systems, to enhance our ability to prevent and respond to agro-terrorism incidents.

In conclusion, access control and perimeter security are vital components of U.S. protection against agro-terrorism. Law enforcement agencies must collaborate with agricultural stakeholders to implement robust security measures, including agro access control protocols, perimeter fortification, advanced surveillance systems, and emergency response protocols. Additionally, international collaborations, public awareness, and research and development efforts are essential in effectively countering the threats of agro-terrorism. By taking a proactive and comprehensive approach, law enforcement agencies can ensure the safety and security of our nation's agricultural resources and food supply chain.

Biosecurity Training for Farm Personnel

In the fight against agro-terrorism and the protection of the nation's food supply chain, it is crucial for law enforcement to work closely with agricultural stakeholders. One of the key areas that require attention is biosecurity training for farm personnel. By equipping those on the front lines of agriculture with the necessary knowledge and skills, we can enhance the overall security of our agricultural infrastructure.

Agricultural biosecurity measures are essential to mitigate the risk of intentional contamination or damage to crops, livestock, and farm facilities. Training farm personnel in these measures is vital to ensure that they can identify potential threats, implement preventive measures, and respond effectively in the event of an agro-terrorism incident.

The training should cover a range of topics, including crop protection technologies and strategies. Farm personnel should be educated on the latest advancements in crop protection, such as integrated pest management techniques and the use of resistant crop varieties. By understanding these strategies, farmers can minimize the impact of pests and diseases, which are potential avenues for agro-terrorism.

Surveillance and monitoring systems for agro-terrorism should also be a core component of the training. Farm personnel should be trained to recognize suspicious activities, unusual pest outbreaks, or signs of unauthorized access to farm facilities. They should understand the importance of reporting such incidents promptly to law enforcement and other relevant authorities.

Emergency response protocols for agro-terrorism incidents should be thoroughly covered in the training as well. Farm personnel should be trained in emergency procedures, including evacuation plans, communication protocols, and the proper handling and containment of potentially hazardous materials. By having well-prepared farm personnel, the response to an agro-terrorism incident can be swift and effective, minimizing the potential damage and ensuring the safety of all involved.

Additionally, the training should include agro-terrorism risk assessment and management. Farm personnel should understand how to identify vulnerabilities in their operations and implement appropriate mitigation measures. This could involve physical security enhancements, such as fencing and access control, as well as employee background checks and awareness programs.

International collaborations in agro-terrorism prevention should also be highlighted in the training. Farm personnel should be made aware of global agro-terrorism threats and the importance of information sharing and cooperation with international partners. By fostering collaboration, we can better detect and prevent potential agro-terrorism incidents before they reach our shores.

Finally, public awareness and education on agro-terrorism threats should be emphasized. Farm personnel should be trained to communicate the importance of biosecurity measures to the general public and engage in outreach initiatives to raise awareness. By involving the public in the fight against agro-terrorism, we can create a collective effort to protect our nation's food supply.

In conclusion, biosecurity training for farm personnel is a critical component of protecting the United States against agro-terrorism. By equipping those in the agricultural sector with the necessary knowledge and skills, we can enhance the overall security of our food supply chain. From crop protection technologies to emergency response protocols, the training should cover a wide range of topics to ensure that farm personnel are well-prepared to detect, prevent, and respond to agro-terrorism incidents. Through international collaborations and public awareness initiatives, we can create a united front in the fight against agro-terrorism and safeguard our agricultural infrastructure.

Biosecurity Measures for Livestock and Poultry Operations

In the face of increasing threats to our food supply chain, it is crucial for law enforcement to understand and implement effective biosecurity measures in livestock and poultry operations. This subchapter aims to provide comprehensive guidance on the importance of securing these operations against agro-terrorism and the steps required to maintain agricultural biosecurity.

Livestock and poultry operations are susceptible to various threats, including intentional acts of agro-terrorism that can have devastating effects on our food supply chain. Therefore, it is imperative for law enforcement agencies to work closely with agricultural stakeholders to develop and enforce robust biosecurity measures.

One of the core aspects of biosecurity in these operations is the implementation of strict access controls. This includes limiting entry to authorized personnel only and maintaining a record of visitors. Additionally, the use of surveillance and monitoring systems can enhance security by providing real-time alerts and deterring potential threats.

Effective emergency response protocols are also essential in mitigating the impact of agro-terrorism incidents. Law enforcement agencies should collaborate with local emergency management authorities and agricultural stakeholders to develop comprehensive plans that address potential scenarios and outline the roles and responsibilities of each party.

Agro-terrorism risk assessment and management should be an ongoing process in livestock and poultry operations. Regular assessments should be conducted to identify vulnerabilities and implement necessary mitigation strategies. This includes training personnel on recognizing and reporting suspicious activities, as well as establishing channels for communication and information sharing between law enforcement agencies and agricultural stakeholders.

International collaborations play a vital role in agro-terrorism prevention. Law enforcement agencies should engage in information exchange and joint exercises with counterparts from other countries to enhance preparedness and response capabilities. Sharing best practices and lessons learned can strengthen our collective ability to combat agro-terrorism threats globally.

Furthermore, public awareness and education are critical components of a comprehensive biosecurity strategy. Law enforcement agencies should actively engage with the public through targeted awareness campaigns to enhance understanding of agro-terrorism threats and encourage reporting of suspicious activities.

Lastly, research and development of advanced detection methods for agro-terrorism are essential to stay ahead of evolving threats. Law enforcement agencies should allocate resources to support research initiatives that focus on developing innovative technologies and strategies to detect and prevent agro-terrorism incidents.

In conclusion, securing livestock and poultry operations against agro-terrorism requires a multi-faceted approach. Law enforcement agencies must collaborate with agricultural stakeholders, implement strict biosecurity measures, develop emergency response protocols, conduct risk assessments, engage in international collaborations, promote public awareness, and invest in research and development. By doing so, we can ensure the protection of our food supply chain and safeguard against the devastating effects of agro-terrorism.

Chapter 4: Food Supply Chain Security

Vulnerabilities in the Food Supply Chain

The food supply chain is a complex and interconnected system that involves multiple stages, from agricultural production to processing, transportation, and distribution. While this system ensures the availability of safe and nutritious food for the population, it also presents various vulnerabilities that can be exploited by individuals or groups with malicious intent. In the context of agro-terrorism, understanding these vulnerabilities is crucial for law enforcement agencies in their role of protecting the United States against potential threats.

One key vulnerability in the food supply chain is the lack of adequate agricultural biosecurity measures. Agricultural facilities, such as farms and processing plants, can be susceptible to unauthorized access, making them potential targets for agro-terrorism. Insufficient biosecurity measures, such as weak fencing or inadequate surveillance systems, increase the risk of contamination or sabotage.

To address this vulnerability, law enforcement agencies need to work closely with the agricultural sector to develop and implement robust biosecurity protocols. This includes conducting risk assessments, strengthening physical security measures, and promoting the use of technology to enhance surveillance and monitoring systems. By ensuring the integrity of agricultural facilities, law enforcement can help safeguard the food supply chain and prevent potential agro-terrorism incidents.

Another vulnerability lies in the transportation and distribution stages of the food supply chain. Food products are often transported over long distances, making them vulnerable to tampering or contamination. Law enforcement agencies should collaborate with transportation companies to develop stringent security protocols, including background checks for employees, secure packaging, and tracking systems to monitor the movement of food products. Additionally, establishing emergency response protocols for agro-terrorism incidents is crucial to minimize the impact and ensure a rapid and coordinated response.

International collaborations also play a significant role in preventing agro-terrorism. Sharing information and best practices with other countries can enhance the collective ability to detect and respond to potential threats. Law enforcement agencies should actively participate in international forums and initiatives focused on agro-terrorism prevention and response, fostering cooperation and intelligence sharing to strengthen global food security.

Furthermore, public awareness and education are essential components of protecting the food supply chain. Law enforcement agencies should engage with the public through campaigns and educational programs that raise awareness about the threats posed by agro-terrorism and the importance of reporting suspicious activities. By empowering individuals to become vigilant and proactive, law enforcement can create a network of eyes and ears that can help detect and prevent potential agro-terrorism incidents.

Finally, research and development of advanced detection methods are critical in staying ahead of evolving agro-terrorism threats. Law enforcement agencies should collaborate with scientific institutions and industry experts to explore innovative technologies and strategies for detecting biological, chemical, or radiological contaminants in food products. By investing in research and development, law enforcement can enhance their capabilities and improve the overall resilience of the food supply chain.

In conclusion, vulnerabilities in the food supply chain pose significant challenges to law enforcement agencies in their role of protecting the United States against agro-terrorism. By addressing these vulnerabilities through the implementation of agricultural biosecurity measures, robust surveillance and monitoring systems, emergency response protocols, and international collaborations, law enforcement can enhance the security of the food supply chain. Additionally, public awareness and education, as well as research and development of advanced detection methods, are vital components in preventing and mitigating agro-terrorism threats. Through a comprehensive and multi-faceted approach, law enforcement agencies can contribute to the overall protection of the nation's food supply and ensure the safety and well-being of its population.

Overview of the Food Supply Chain

The food supply chain is a complex network of interconnected processes and systems that ensure the safe and efficient production, processing, distribution, and consumption of food. This subchapter provides an overview of the food supply chain, highlighting its importance for national security and the role of law enforcement in protecting it against agro-terrorism.

The food supply chain begins with the production of crops and livestock on farms and ranches across the country. These agricultural operations are vulnerable to various threats, including natural disasters, pests, diseases, and deliberate acts of agro-terrorism. Agricultural biosecurity measures, such as strict biosecurity protocols, vaccination programs, and pest control strategies, are essential to protect the integrity of the food supply chain.

Once the agricultural products are harvested, they undergo processing and packaging in facilities such as food processing plants and slaughterhouses. These facilities must adhere to strict hygiene and safety standards to prevent contamination and ensure the quality of the products. Law enforcement plays a crucial role in monitoring and enforcing compliance with these standards to safeguard the integrity of the food supply chain.

The next stage of the food supply chain involves the transportation and distribution of the processed food products to various retail outlets, restaurants, and consumers. Food supply chain security is vital at this stage to prevent tampering, theft, or sabotage of the products. Law enforcement agencies collaborate with transportation companies and logistics providers to implement surveillance and monitoring systems that detect any suspicious activities or unauthorized access to the food products.

In the event of an agro-terrorism incident or any other emergency that poses a risk to the food supply chain, it is crucial to have well-defined emergency response protocols in place. Law enforcement agencies work closely with other stakeholders, including government agencies, emergency management organizations, and industry partners, to develop and implement these protocols. This ensures a coordinated and effective response to mitigate the impact of such incidents and restore the integrity of the food supply chain.

Agro-terrorism risk assessment and management is an ongoing process that involves identifying potential threats, evaluating their likelihood and consequences, and implementing measures to mitigate the risks. Law enforcement agencies collaborate with agricultural experts, intelligence agencies, and other relevant stakeholders to conduct risk assessments and develop strategies to prevent and respond to agro-terrorism incidents.

Protecting the agricultural infrastructure, including farms, processing facilities, storage facilities, and transportation networks, is an essential aspect of securing the food supply chain. Law enforcement agencies play a vital role in patrolling and monitoring these critical infrastructures to prevent unauthorized access, vandalism, or sabotage.

International collaborations are crucial in preventing agro-terrorism. Law enforcement agencies work closely with their international counterparts to share intelligence, best practices, and technologies to enhance the security of the global food supply chain.

Public awareness and education are vital in ensuring the cooperation and support of the public in preventing and responding to agro-terrorism threats. Law enforcement agencies engage in outreach programs and public awareness campaigns to educate the public about the risks of agro-terrorism and the importance of reporting any suspicious activities related to the food supply chain.

Research and development of advanced detection methods for agro-terrorism are ongoing efforts to stay ahead of evolving threats. Law enforcement agencies collaborate with research institutions and technology providers to develop innovative technologies and strategies for early detection and prevention of agro-terrorism incidents.

In conclusion, the food supply chain is a critical component of national security, and law enforcement plays a crucial role in protecting it against agro-terrorism. By understanding the various stages of the supply chain and implementing measures such as agricultural biosecurity, surveillance systems, emergency response protocols, risk assessment, and international collaborations, law enforcement agencies can effectively safeguard the integrity and safety of the food supply chain.

Potential Agro-Terrorist Targets within the Food Supply Chain

As law enforcement officials, it is crucial to understand the potential targets within the food supply chain that could be vulnerable to agro-terrorism. Agro-terrorism refers to acts of terrorism aimed at disrupting or damaging the agricultural industry and food supply. Such acts can have severe consequences for public health, economic stability, and national security. Therefore, it is imperative that law enforcement agencies stay informed and prepared to protect against these threats.

One of the primary targets within the food supply chain is the agricultural infrastructure itself. This includes farms, processing plants, and storage facilities. These locations are vulnerable to attacks aimed at contaminating crops or livestock, which could result in the release of harmful pathogens or toxins into the food supply. Law enforcement must collaborate with agricultural stakeholders to ensure the security and protection of these critical assets.

Another target is the transportation system that moves food from farms to consumers. Agro-terrorists may attempt to disrupt the supply chain by targeting trucks, railways, or ports, leading to delays, spoilage, or contamination of goods in transit. Law enforcement agencies need to work closely with transportation authorities to implement surveillance and monitoring systems to detect any suspicious activities and prevent potential attacks.

Crop protection technologies and strategies are essential in safeguarding against agro-terrorism. Law enforcement must support research and development efforts to advance detection methods for agro-terrorism. This includes the use of advanced sensors, drones, and satellite imagery to monitor crops for signs of contamination or disease. By staying on the cutting edge of technology, law enforcement can enhance their ability to identify and respond to potential threats.

Emergency response protocols are critical in mitigating the impact of agro-terrorism incidents. Law enforcement agencies should establish clear procedures for coordinating with other agencies, such as public health departments and emergency management teams, to ensure a swift and effective response. Regular drills and training exercises should be conducted to test and refine these protocols.

International collaborations play a vital role in agro-terrorism prevention. Law enforcement agencies should work closely with their international counterparts to share intelligence, best practices, and resources. By fostering these collaborations, we can enhance global efforts to detect and prevent agro-terrorism threats.

Public awareness and education are key in mitigating agro-terrorism risks. Law enforcement agencies should engage in outreach programs to educate the public about the potential threats and the importance of reporting any suspicious activities. By empowering the public, we can create a network of vigilant citizens who can aid in early detection and prevention efforts.

In conclusion, law enforcement's role in protecting against agro-terrorism is critical. By understanding the potential targets within the food supply chain, collaborating with agricultural stakeholders, implementing surveillance and monitoring systems, developing emergency response protocols, and engaging in international collaborations, law enforcement can effectively mitigate the risks posed by agro-terrorism. Through public awareness and education, law enforcement agencies can empower the public to be proactive in reporting suspicious activities. With continued research and development, law enforcement can stay ahead of evolving threats and protect America's harvest.

Ensuring Food Supply Chain Security

The security of the food supply chain is of paramount importance to safeguard public health, maintain economic stability, and protect national security. With the increasing threat of agro-terrorism, it is crucial for law enforcement agencies to play a vital role in the protection of the United States against such attacks. This subchapter aims to provide key insights and strategies for law enforcement professionals to enhance the security of the food supply chain.

To effectively protect the food supply chain, it is imperative to implement comprehensive agricultural biosecurity measures. This includes strict regulations and inspections at all stages of production, processing, and distribution. Law enforcement agencies should collaborate with agricultural stakeholders to ensure compliance with these measures and prevent any potential threats.

Crop protection technologies and strategies are essential in mitigating the risk of agro-terrorism. Law enforcement agencies should stay abreast of the latest advancements in this field to provide guidance and support to farmers and agricultural businesses. Additionally, investing in surveillance and monitoring systems specifically designed to detect agro-terrorism threats can significantly enhance the overall security of the food supply chain.

Emergency response protocols for agro-terrorism incidents should be well-established and regularly practiced to minimize the impact of an attack. Law enforcement agencies must work closely with other relevant agencies and organizations to develop effective response plans and facilitate a coordinated effort in case of an emergency.

Agro-terrorism risk assessment and management are vital components in proactively identifying vulnerabilities and implementing preventive measures. Law enforcement agencies should collaborate with experts in the field to conduct thorough risk assessments and develop strategies to mitigate potential threats.

The protection of agricultural infrastructure is crucial to maintain a secure food supply chain. Law enforcement agencies should work in close partnership with agricultural stakeholders to identify critical infrastructure and develop measures to protect them from potential attacks.

International collaborations in agro-terrorism prevention are necessary to tackle this global threat effectively. Law enforcement agencies should foster partnerships with international counterparts, share information, and coordinate efforts to enhance the security of the food supply chain on a global scale.

Public awareness and education play a pivotal role in preventing agro-terrorism. Law enforcement agencies should engage in outreach programs to educate the public, farmers, and agricultural businesses about the threats posed by agro-terrorism and the necessary preventive measures.

Research and development of advanced detection methods for agro-terrorism are crucial to stay ahead of evolving threats. Law enforcement agencies should support and collaborate with research institutions to develop innovative technologies and techniques for early detection and prevention of agro-terrorism incidents.

By prioritizing the security of the food supply chain, law enforcement agencies can effectively contribute to the protection of the United States against agro-terrorism. Through collaboration, education, and the implementation of advanced technologies, the threat of agro-terrorism can be mitigated, ensuring a safe and secure food supply for the nation.

Supply Chain Risk Assessment and Management

Supply chain risk assessment and management are critical components in ensuring the security of the U.S. food supply against agro-terrorism threats. Law enforcement plays a pivotal role in identifying, assessing, and mitigating these risks to safeguard the nation's agricultural resources and protect public health.

Agro-terrorism poses significant challenges to the U.S. food supply chain, which encompasses the production, processing, distribution, and consumption of agricultural products. To effectively manage these risks, it is essential to conduct comprehensive risk assessments that encompass all stages of the supply chain.

The first step in supply chain risk assessment is identifying potential vulnerabilities. This involves evaluating the entire system, including physical infrastructure, transportation networks, storage facilities, and information systems. Law enforcement agencies must work closely with industry stakeholders to gather intelligence and identify potential weak points susceptible to agro-terrorism attacks.

Once vulnerabilities are identified, risk assessment methodologies can be applied to quantify the likelihood and consequences of potential threats. This includes analyzing the impact of disruptions on the availability, quality, and safety of agricultural products. By understanding the potential risks, law enforcement can develop targeted strategies to mitigate their impact.

Supply chain risk management involves implementing measures to prevent, detect, and respond to agro-terrorism incidents. This includes the adoption of agricultural biosecurity measures, such as strict access controls, surveillance systems, and employee training programs. Law enforcement agencies should collaborate with relevant stakeholders to develop emergency response protocols specific to agro-terrorism incidents, ensuring a coordinated and efficient response.

Furthermore, international collaborations play a crucial role in preventing agro-terrorism. Sharing intelligence, best practices, and technological advancements with global partners enhances the collective ability to detect and prevent attacks on the agricultural sector. Law enforcement agencies should actively engage in such collaborations to strengthen the nation's defense against agro-terrorism threats.

Public awareness and education are also vital in combating agro-terrorism. By informing the public about the potential risks and encouraging reporting of suspicious activities, law enforcement can gain valuable intelligence and enhance the overall security posture.

Finally, continuous research and development of advanced detection methods are key to staying ahead of evolving agro-terrorism threats. By investing in innovative crop protection technologies, surveillance and monitoring systems, and early warning systems, law enforcement can proactively detect and prevent potential attacks.

In conclusion, supply chain risk assessment and management are essential in protecting the U.S. against agro-terrorism. Law enforcement agencies must collaborate with industry stakeholders, develop comprehensive risk assessment methodologies, implement preventive measures, and enhance international collaborations to ensure the security of the nation's food supply. By prioritizing public awareness and investing in research and development, law enforcement can effectively mitigate agro-terrorism risks and safeguard the agricultural sector.

Tracking and Traceability Systems

In the fight against agro-terrorism, law enforcement plays a crucial role in ensuring the security and protection of America's harvest. One of the key tools at their disposal is the implementation of tracking and traceability systems. These systems are designed to monitor and trace the movement of agricultural products throughout the entire supply chain, from farm to fork. By implementing robust tracking and traceability systems, law enforcement can enhance their ability to identify and respond to potential agro-terrorism threats.

Tracking and traceability systems involve the use of advanced technologies and strategies to track the movement of agricultural products. This includes the use of barcode systems, radio frequency identification (RFID) tags, and other unique identifiers that enable the seamless monitoring of products from their origin to their final destination. These systems not only provide valuable information about the origin and journey of agricultural products but also help identify and address any potential security breaches or contamination risks.

By integrating tracking and traceability systems into the agricultural biosecurity measures, law enforcement can effectively monitor the entire food supply chain. This includes tracking the movement of livestock, crops, and other agricultural products, as well as monitoring the transportation and storage facilities involved. By doing so, law enforcement can quickly identify any suspicious activities or deviations from established protocols, allowing them to respond swiftly and mitigate potential agro-terrorism threats.

Surveillance and monitoring systems are a critical component of tracking and traceability systems. Through the use of advanced surveillance technologies such as CCTV cameras, drones, and satellite imagery, law enforcement can continuously monitor agricultural areas and critical infrastructure for any signs of unauthorized activities or potential threats. These systems can also be integrated with real-time data analysis and alert systems, enabling law enforcement to respond promptly to any suspicious activities or incidents.

In the event of an agro-terrorism incident, tracking and traceability systems provide essential information for emergency response protocols. By quickly identifying the source of contamination or tampering, law enforcement can take immediate action to contain the threat, minimize the impact on public health, and maintain the integrity of the agricultural industry.

International collaborations in the prevention of agro-terrorism are also facilitated by tracking and traceability systems. By adopting standardized tracking and traceability protocols, countries can share critical information and intelligence, enhancing their collective ability to prevent and respond to agro-terrorism threats. These collaborations also enable the exchange of best practices and the development of advanced detection methods, strengthening the overall security of the global agricultural industry.

Public awareness and education on agro-terrorism threats are essential in ensuring the effectiveness of tracking and traceability systems. By educating farmers, food manufacturers, and the general public about the importance of these systems, law enforcement can foster a culture of vigilance and encourage proactive reporting of any suspicious activities or incidents. Public awareness campaigns can also help dispel misinformation and rumors, ensuring that accurate information is disseminated in the event of an agro-terrorism incident.

Research and development of advanced detection methods for agro-terrorism are crucial for the continuous improvement of tracking and traceability systems. By investing in the development of innovative technologies and strategies, law enforcement can stay ahead of evolving agro-terrorism threats. This includes the use of emerging technologies such as blockchain and artificial intelligence to enhance the accuracy and efficiency of tracking and traceability systems.

In conclusion, tracking and traceability systems are vital tools in law enforcement's efforts to protect America's harvest from agro-terrorism. By integrating these systems into the agricultural biosecurity measures, law enforcement can enhance their ability to monitor, respond to, and mitigate potential threats. Through international collaborations, public awareness, and continuous research and development, law enforcement can stay one step ahead in the fight against agro-terrorism.

Collaboration with Food Industry Stakeholders

In the fight against agro-terrorism, collaboration with food industry stakeholders is crucial for ensuring the protection of America's harvest and securing the nation's food supply chain. Law enforcement agencies play a vital role in fostering these collaborations and working alongside industry professionals to mitigate the risks associated with agro-terrorism.

One of the key areas of collaboration is agricultural biosecurity measures. By partnering with farmers, ranchers, and agricultural workers, law enforcement agencies can develop and implement biosecurity protocols to prevent the introduction and spread of diseases, pests, and other threats to crops and livestock. This collaboration can involve training programs, sharing of best practices, and joint exercises to enhance preparedness and response capabilities.

Another important aspect of collaboration is food supply chain security. Law enforcement agencies can work closely with food producers, processors, distributors, and retailers to identify vulnerabilities in the supply chain and implement measures to protect it from potential terrorist attacks. This collaboration can involve conducting risk assessments, developing security plans, and sharing intelligence on potential threats or suspicious activities.

Crop protection technologies and strategies are also areas where collaboration with industry stakeholders is essential. Law enforcement agencies can collaborate with agricultural researchers and technology developers to identify and deploy innovative technologies for crop protection, such as advanced surveillance systems, drone technology, and remote sensing. By working together, law enforcement and industry professionals can stay at the forefront of technological advancements to counter agro-terrorism threats effectively.

Surveillance and monitoring systems for agro-terrorism are critical in detecting and preventing attacks. Collaboration with industry stakeholders, such as agricultural associations and private security firms, can help law enforcement agencies establish effective surveillance and monitoring systems. By sharing resources, expertise, and information, these partnerships can enhance the ability to detect suspicious activities, identify potential threats, and respond swiftly to agro-terrorism incidents.

Emergency response protocols for agro-terrorism incidents require coordination and collaboration with various stakeholders, including food industry professionals. By working together, law enforcement agencies and industry stakeholders can develop comprehensive response plans, conduct joint training exercises, and establish communication channels to ensure a coordinated and effective response in the event of an agro-terrorism incident.

Collaboration is also crucial in agro-terrorism risk assessment and management. Law enforcement agencies can work closely with agricultural experts, researchers, and industry professionals to assess vulnerabilities, develop risk mitigation strategies, and prioritize resources for prevention and response efforts. This collaboration can involve sharing data, conducting joint assessments, and developing intelligence networks to stay ahead of emerging threats.

International collaborations in agro-terrorism prevention are essential for addressing the global nature of the threat. Law enforcement agencies can collaborate with international partners, such as intelligence agencies, law enforcement agencies, and agricultural organizations, to share information, conduct joint investigations, and develop coordinated strategies to prevent and respond to agro-terrorism incidents.

Public awareness and education on agro-terrorism threats are vital in engaging the public and fostering a sense of shared responsibility. Law enforcement agencies can collaborate with food industry stakeholders to develop outreach programs, educational materials, and public awareness campaigns to inform citizens, farmers, and consumers about the risks of agro-terrorism and the importance of vigilance and reporting suspicious activities.

Lastly, research and development of advanced detection methods for agro-terrorism require collaboration with industry stakeholders. By partnering with agricultural researchers, technology developers, and private companies, law enforcement agencies can support the development and deployment of cutting-edge detection technologies, such as biosensors, nanotechnology, and imaging systems, to enhance the ability to detect and prevent agro-terrorism threats.

In conclusion, collaboration with food industry stakeholders is essential for law enforcement agencies in the fight against agro-terrorism. By working together, law enforcement and industry professionals can enhance agricultural biosecurity measures, strengthen food supply chain security, develop advanced crop protection technologies and strategies, establish effective surveillance and monitoring systems, implement emergency response protocols, conduct agro-terrorism risk assessments, protect agricultural infrastructure, foster international collaborations, promote public awareness and education, and support research and development of advanced detection methods. These collaborations are crucial for securing America's harvest and ensuring the nation's protection against agro-terrorism.

Chapter 5: Crop Protection Technologies and Strategies

Integrated Pest Management (IPM)

Integrated Pest Management (IPM) is a comprehensive approach to crop protection that aims to minimize the use of pesticides while effectively managing pests and reducing the risk of agro-terrorism. This subchapter will provide law enforcement officials with an overview of IPM strategies and their role in implementing and supporting these measures to safeguard the U.S. food supply chain.

IPM is based on the principles of prevention, monitoring, and control. It emphasizes the use of a combination of techniques, including biological control, cultural practices, and chemical interventions, to manage pests effectively. By integrating these strategies, IPM reduces the reliance on pesticides, which can be attractive targets for agro-terrorists seeking to disrupt agricultural production and compromise food safety.

Law enforcement agencies play a crucial role in supporting IPM practices by enforcing regulations related to the use and storage of pesticides, investigating suspicious activities, and collaborating with agricultural stakeholders to enhance security measures. By working closely with farmers, agricultural extension services, and researchers, law enforcement officials can help identify potential vulnerabilities and develop targeted responses to agro-terrorism threats.

Surveillance and monitoring systems are essential components of IPM and agro-terrorism prevention. Law enforcement agencies should be aware of the various surveillance technologies available, such as remote sensing, drones, and satellite imagery, which can aid in early pest detection and response. These systems can also be utilized to enhance security in critical agricultural infrastructure, such as storage facilities and processing plants.

In the event of an agro-terrorism incident, law enforcement must be prepared to respond swiftly and effectively. Emergency response protocols should be established, clearly outlining the roles and responsibilities of different agencies and stakeholders. Training programs should be implemented to ensure that law enforcement officials are equipped with the necessary knowledge and skills to handle such incidents, including evidence collection, risk assessment, and coordination with other agencies.

International collaborations are crucial in agro-terrorism prevention, as threats to the U.S. food supply chain can originate from both domestic and foreign sources. Law enforcement agencies should actively engage with international partners to share information, intelligence, and best practices. Collaboration can also extend to research and development efforts, focusing on advanced detection methods for agro-terrorism.

Public awareness and education on agro-terrorism threats are vital in building a resilient agricultural sector. Law enforcement agencies should actively engage with the public, agricultural communities, and educational institutions to raise awareness about the potential risks and the importance of implementing biosecurity measures. By fostering a culture of vigilance and preparedness, law enforcement can contribute to the overall security of the U.S. food supply chain.

In conclusion, Integrated Pest Management (IPM) is an essential component of U.S. protection against agro-terrorism. Law enforcement agencies play a critical role in supporting IPM practices, ensuring compliance with regulations, enhancing surveillance and monitoring systems, coordinating emergency responses, and collaborating with international partners. By effectively implementing IPM strategies and promoting public awareness, law enforcement can contribute to the safeguarding of the U.S. agricultural sector from agro-terrorism threats, ensuring a secure and sustainable food supply chain for the nation.

Principles and Benefits of IPM

Integrated Pest Management (IPM) is a comprehensive approach to crop protection that focuses on sustainable practices and minimizes reliance on chemical pesticides. This subchapter explores the principles and benefits of IPM in the context of U.S. protection against agro-terrorism, highlighting its importance for law enforcement and the various niches involved in agro-terrorism prevention.

The principles of IPM involve the integration of multiple strategies to manage pests effectively while minimizing risks to human health and the environment. These strategies include biological control, cultural practices, habitat manipulation, crop rotation, and the judicious use of pesticides when necessary. By combining these approaches, IPM aims to maintain pest populations below economically damaging levels while reducing the reliance on chemical pesticides.

The benefits of IPM in the context of agro-terrorism prevention are significant. Firstly, IPM promotes the long-term sustainability of agriculture by reducing the development of pesticide resistance and preserving beneficial organisms that help control pests. This is particularly crucial in the face of potential agro-terrorism attacks that may target specific crops or regions, as IPM allows for a more resilient and adaptable agricultural system.

Secondly, IPM enhances food supply chain security by ensuring the production of safe and high-quality food. By utilizing a range of pest management strategies, IPM minimizes the risks of pesticide residues in food products, thus safeguarding public health. This is of utmost importance in the event of an agro-terrorism incident, as contaminated food can have severe consequences for both consumers and the economy.

Furthermore, IPM aligns with the principles of surveillance and monitoring systems for agro-terrorism. By implementing IPM practices, law enforcement can identify and track pest populations more effectively, enabling early detection and targeted response to potential threats. This proactive approach is essential for protecting agricultural infrastructure and preventing the spread of agro-terrorism incidents.

Lastly, IPM encourages international collaborations in agro-terrorism prevention. The principles and practices of IPM are applicable across borders, making it a valuable tool for sharing knowledge and expertise in the fight against agro-terrorism. By promoting the adoption of IPM globally, law enforcement agencies can work together to build a more secure and resilient agricultural system.

In conclusion, the principles and benefits of IPM are paramount in the protection against agro-terrorism. By embracing IPM, law enforcement agencies, agricultural stakeholders, and the wider public can contribute to a more sustainable, secure, and resilient food supply chain. Through the integration of various strategies and the reduction of chemical pesticide reliance, IPM serves as a crucial component in the prevention and response to agro-terrorism incidents.

Implementing IPM Practices for Agro-Terrorism Prevention

Introduction:

As the threat of agro-terrorism continues to loom over the United States, it is crucial for law enforcement agencies to play an active role in protecting the nation's agricultural sector. One effective approach to counter this threat is the implementation of Integrated Pest Management (IPM) practices. IPM combines various strategies to minimize the risks posed by pests, diseases, and potential agro-terrorism incidents. This subchapter explores the importance of IPM practices in preventing agro-terrorism and highlights its relevance to law enforcement agencies.

Understanding IPM and its Role:

IPM is a comprehensive approach that integrates multiple pest management techniques to reduce reliance on chemical pesticides while effectively managing pest populations. By implementing IPM practices, law enforcement agencies can contribute to the prevention of agro-terrorism by safeguarding the agricultural biosecurity measures, food supply chain security, and crop protection technologies and strategies.

Surveillance and Monitoring Systems:

IPM emphasizes the importance of surveillance and monitoring systems to detect and respond to potential agro-terrorism threats. Law enforcement agencies can collaborate with agricultural stakeholders to develop and implement advanced surveillance technologies, such as drones, satellite imagery, and data analytics, to monitor crops, identify invasive species, and track potential agro-terrorism activities.

Emergency Response Protocols:

In the event of an agro-terrorism incident, law enforcement agencies must be prepared to respond swiftly and effectively. IPM practices can provide valuable guidance in developing emergency response protocols specific to agro-terrorism incidents. These protocols should encompass measures to contain the spread of pests or diseases, secure affected areas, and coordinate with relevant agencies to mitigate the impact on agricultural infrastructure and the food supply chain.

Risk Assessment and Management:

IPM practices also support agro-terrorism risk assessment and management. By conducting thorough risk assessments, law enforcement agencies can identify vulnerabilities in the agricultural sector and develop targeted strategies to mitigate those risks. IPM's holistic approach can aid in identifying potential entry points for agro-terrorism activities, evaluating the effectiveness of existing security measures, and implementing preventive measures to reduce vulnerabilities.

Public Awareness and Education:

Law enforcement agencies play a vital role in raising public awareness about the threats posed by agro-terrorism and the importance of implementing IPM practices. By engaging with stakeholders, conducting outreach programs, and disseminating information, law enforcement agencies can educate the public on the significance of securing America's harvest and the need for collaborative efforts in agro-terrorism prevention.

Conclusion:

Implementing IPM practices is an integral part of law enforcement's role in protecting the United States against agro-terrorism. By integrating IPM strategies into their operations, law enforcement agencies can contribute to agricultural biosecurity, maintain food supply chain security, and effectively respond to agro-terrorism incidents. Collaboration with agricultural stakeholders, international partners, and research institutions will further enhance the development and implementation of advanced detection methods to counter agro-terrorism threats. Together, law enforcement agencies and the broader agricultural community can ensure the resilience and security of America's agricultural sector.

Genetic Modification and Biotechnology in Crop Protection

In recent years, genetic modification and biotechnology have emerged as powerful tools in the field of crop protection. With the increasing threat of agro-terrorism and the need for robust agricultural biosecurity measures, these technologies offer innovative solutions for safeguarding the U.S. food supply chain and protecting against potential agro-terrorism incidents.

One of the key advantages of genetic modification is its ability to enhance the inherent resistance of crops to pests, diseases, and environmental stressors. Through the insertion of specific genes, crops can be engineered to produce natural insecticides or to be resistant to certain pathogens. This not only reduces the reliance on chemical pesticides but also minimizes the risk of contamination and adverse effects on human health and the environment.

Biotechnology, on the other hand, encompasses a broader range of techniques, such as tissue culture, molecular markers, and genetic fingerprinting, which are crucial for surveillance and monitoring systems for agro-terrorism. These tools enable rapid and accurate identification of potential threats, facilitating early detection and response to agro-terrorism incidents.

In addition to crop protection technologies, it is essential to establish effective emergency response protocols for agro-terrorism incidents. Law enforcement plays a critical role in coordinating and executing these response efforts, working closely with agricultural stakeholders, biosecurity experts, and first responders. Timely and coordinated actions are necessary to minimize the impact of agro-terrorism on the food supply chain and ensure public safety.

Agro-terrorism risk assessment and management also require close collaboration between law enforcement agencies and agricultural experts. By leveraging their respective expertise, they can identify vulnerabilities in the agricultural infrastructure and develop strategies to mitigate potential risks. This includes implementing enhanced physical security measures, conducting regular inspections and audits, and promoting information sharing and intelligence gathering.

International collaborations are crucial in the prevention of agro-terrorism. Given the global nature of the agriculture and food industries, it is imperative to establish partnerships with other countries to share best practices, intelligence, and research findings. By working together, law enforcement agencies can enhance their capacity to detect, prevent, and respond to agro-terrorism incidents effectively.

Public awareness and education on agro-terrorism threats are equally important. Law enforcement agencies should engage in outreach programs to educate farmers, agricultural workers, and the general public about the potential risks and the measures in place to protect the food supply chain. This will not only promote vigilance but also foster a sense of shared responsibility in safeguarding the nation's agricultural resources.

To stay ahead of the ever-evolving challenges posed by agro-terrorism, continuous research and development of advanced detection methods are vital. Law enforcement agencies should collaborate with scientists, researchers, and technology developers to explore innovative solutions and technologies, such as remote sensing, drones, and artificial intelligence, to enhance surveillance capabilities and early detection of potential agro-terrorism threats.

In conclusion, genetic modification and biotechnology offer promising avenues for crop protection in the face of agro-terrorism. By leveraging these technologies, law enforcement agencies can strengthen the U.S. protection against agro-terrorism, safeguard the agricultural biosecurity measures, ensure food supply chain security, and establish effective surveillance, monitoring, and emergency response protocols. Furthermore, international collaborations, public awareness, and research and development efforts are essential components in the comprehensive strategy to prevent agro-terrorism and protect the nation's agricultural infrastructure.

Role of Genetic Modification in Enhancing Crop Resistance

The Role of Genetic Modification in Enhancing Crop Resistance

Genetic modification (GM) has emerged as a significant tool in the field of agriculture, playing a crucial role in enhancing crop resistance against various threats. This subchapter explores the application of genetic modification and its potential in securing America's harvest, with a particular focus on the role of law enforcement in protecting the United States against agro-terrorism.

One of the primary objectives of genetic modification is to develop crops that are resistant to pests, diseases, and environmental stresses. By introducing specific genes into crop plants, scientists have been able to enhance their natural defense mechanisms, making them more resilient to various threats. This technology has proven particularly valuable in safeguarding the food supply chain and ensuring food security for the nation.

Law enforcement agencies play a critical role in the protection against agro-terrorism, which involves intentional acts of sabotage or contamination of agricultural resources. The integration of genetic modification strategies in crop protection technologies and strategies can significantly aid law enforcement in their efforts. By implementing advanced surveillance and monitoring systems for agro-terrorism, law enforcement can detect any suspicious activities and respond promptly to mitigate potential threats.

Moreover, genetic modification enables the development of crops with built-in detection mechanisms, allowing law enforcement to quickly identify and trace any contaminated produce within the food supply chain. This can be instrumental in preventing the spread of harmful substances and minimizing the impact on public health.

Emergency response protocols for agro-terrorism incidents can also benefit from the advancements in genetic modification. By utilizing genetically modified crops that exhibit enhanced resistance, law enforcement can quickly stabilize the situation and limit the damage caused by agro-terrorism incidents. These protocols should be well-coordinated and integrated with local, state, and federal agencies to ensure a swift and effective response.

Furthermore, genetic modification can contribute to agro-terrorism risk assessment and management. By conducting in-depth studies and research, law enforcement can determine the vulnerabilities in the agricultural infrastructure and develop strategies to address them. This can help identify potential targets for agro-terrorism and devise preventive measures to protect critical agricultural resources.

International collaborations in agro-terrorism prevention are also crucial, and genetic modification can play a significant role in fostering such partnerships. By sharing expertise, knowledge, and resources, nations can collectively work towards securing global food systems from agro-terrorism threats. Law enforcement agencies should actively participate in these collaborations to leverage genetic modification and other advanced detection methods to enhance security measures.

Finally, public awareness and education on agro-terrorism threats are essential in ensuring the success of preventive efforts. Law enforcement agencies should actively engage with the public, disseminating information on the benefits and safety of genetic modification, and addressing any concerns or misconceptions. By fostering public trust and understanding, law enforcement can gain support for their initiatives and strengthen the overall security of the agricultural sector.

In conclusion, genetic modification holds immense potential in enhancing crop resistance and protecting the United States against agro-terrorism. Law enforcement agencies should actively collaborate with agricultural and scientific communities to leverage genetic modification and other advanced technologies in securing America's harvest. By integrating these strategies, law enforcement can significantly contribute to the protection of the nation's agricultural resources and ensure the safety and security of the food supply chain.

Controversies and Public Perception of Genetically Modified Organisms (GMOs)

In recent years, the use of genetically modified organisms (GMOs) in agriculture has sparked numerous controversies and raised concerns among the public. As law enforcement officers involved in the protection against agro-terrorism, it is essential to understand the controversies surrounding GMOs and the public perception of this technology.

GMOs refer to organisms whose genetic material has been modified through genetic engineering techniques. These modifications are aimed at enhancing certain desirable traits, such as increased resistance to pests, diseases, or herbicides. While GMOs have been widely adopted in modern agriculture to improve crop yields and reduce reliance on chemical inputs, they have faced criticism and skepticism from various stakeholders.

One of the primary concerns surrounding GMOs is their potential impact on human health and the environment. Critics argue that the long-term effects of consuming genetically modified foods are still unknown and may pose risks to human health. Additionally, there are concerns about the potential for GMOs to crossbreed with wild relatives and disrupt natural ecosystems.

Furthermore, GMOs have raised ethical and socio-economic concerns. Some critics argue that genetic modification interferes with nature and violates the sanctity of natural organisms. Others believe that GMOs contribute to corporate control of the food supply, as large biotech companies hold patents on genetically modified seeds, limiting farmers' freedom to save and replant seeds.

Public perception of GMOs varies widely, with some individuals embracing the technology for its potential to address global food security challenges, while others are deeply skeptical and even hostile towards GMOs. This diversity of opinions can complicate the enforcement of laws related to agro-terrorism incidents involving GMOs, as public support and cooperation are essential for effective law enforcement action.

As law enforcement officers, it is crucial to remain neutral and unbiased when dealing with GMO-related controversies. Understanding the concerns and perspectives of various stakeholders is essential for effective communication and collaboration. It is equally important to stay updated with the latest scientific research and regulatory frameworks surrounding GMOs to ensure informed decision-making when addressing agro-terrorism incidents involving GMOs.

In conclusion, controversies and public perception of genetically modified organisms (GMOs) play a significant role in the landscape of agro-terrorism prevention and response. As law enforcement officers involved in protecting the US against agro-terrorism, understanding these controversies and public perception is vital for effective communication, collaboration, and decision-making in this field.

Chapter 6: Surveillance and Monitoring Systems for Agro-Terrorism

Importance of Surveillance and Monitoring

Surveillance and monitoring play a vital role in safeguarding the United States against agro-terrorism threats. In the book "Securing America's Harvest: Law Enforcement's Role in U.S. Protection Against Agro-Terrorism," this subchapter aims to highlight the significance of robust surveillance and monitoring systems in ensuring agricultural biosecurity, food supply chain security, and efficient crop protection technologies and strategies.

Law enforcement agencies have a critical responsibility in preventing and responding to agro-terrorism incidents. By implementing effective surveillance and monitoring systems, these agencies can proactively identify potential threats and mitigate risks. Surveillance allows for the continuous observation of vulnerable areas, such as farms, agricultural facilities, and critical infrastructure. Through the use of advanced technologies, including drones, satellites, and sensors, law enforcement can detect suspicious activities, unauthorized access, or any other signs of potential agro-terrorism.

Monitoring systems are equally crucial in maintaining the integrity of the food supply chain. By closely monitoring the transportation, processing, and storage of agricultural products, law enforcement can identify any tampering or contamination attempts. This helps ensure that only safe and secure products reach consumers, protecting public health and preventing economic disruptions.

Moreover, surveillance and monitoring systems enable law enforcement to gather valuable intelligence on agro-terrorism threats. By analyzing patterns, trends, and behaviors, agencies can identify potential perpetrators, their modus operandi, and any emerging tactics. This intelligence can inform risk assessment and management strategies, allowing law enforcement to allocate resources effectively and prioritize response efforts.

In the event of an agro-terrorism incident, surveillance and monitoring systems play a crucial role in emergency response protocols. Real-time data and surveillance footage help law enforcement agencies coordinate their response, deploy resources, and communicate with relevant stakeholders. By promptly identifying the source and extent of the incident, law enforcement can minimize the impact on agricultural production, public safety, and the economy.

To ensure continuous improvement in agro-terrorism prevention, law enforcement should also focus on research and development of advanced detection methods. By investing in cutting-edge technologies and collaborating with experts in the field, agencies can enhance their surveillance and monitoring capabilities. This includes exploring innovations in remote sensing, big data analytics, and artificial intelligence to detect and respond to agro-terrorism threats swiftly.

In conclusion, the importance of surveillance and monitoring in protecting the United States against agro-terrorism cannot be overstated. Law enforcement agencies must recognize the significance of robust surveillance systems in the context of agricultural biosecurity, food supply chain security, and crop protection technologies. By implementing advanced surveillance and monitoring systems, law enforcement can effectively prevent, detect, and respond to agro-terrorism incidents. This subchapter aims to provide law enforcement professionals with valuable insights and strategies to enhance surveillance and monitoring efforts, ensuring the safety and security of America's agricultural sector.

Early Detection and Rapid Response

Early detection and rapid response are crucial elements in the fight against agro-terrorism. As law enforcement professionals, it is imperative to understand the significance of these factors and their role in protecting the United States against agro-terrorism threats.

Agricultural biosecurity measures play a vital role in preventing and mitigating agro-terrorism incidents. By implementing strict biosecurity protocols, such as securing farm premises, controlling access to sensitive areas, and monitoring the movement of livestock and agricultural products, law enforcement can effectively deter potential agro-terrorist activities.

Another critical aspect is ensuring food supply chain security. Law enforcement should collaborate with key stakeholders, including farmers, food processors, distributors, and retailers, to establish robust security measures throughout the entire supply chain. Regular inspections, audits, and strict adherence to traceability protocols can help identify any potential threats early on.

Crop protection technologies and strategies are constantly evolving, and it is essential for law enforcement to stay up-to-date with the latest advancements. By understanding and utilizing innovative technologies like drone surveillance, satellite imaging, and remote sensing, law enforcement can enhance their surveillance and monitoring systems for agro-terrorism. These technologies enable early detection of suspicious activities, allowing for a rapid response to potential threats.

In the event of an agro-terrorism incident, law enforcement must have well-defined emergency response protocols in place. This includes establishing clear communication channels, coordinating with relevant agencies, and training personnel to effectively respond to such incidents. Regular drills and exercises can help ensure a swift and coordinated response, minimizing the impact of agro-terrorism on agricultural infrastructure and public safety.

Agro-terrorism risk assessment and management are crucial for effective prevention. Law enforcement should work closely with agricultural experts and intelligence agencies to identify potential targets, assess vulnerabilities, and develop risk management strategies. This proactive approach can help prevent agro-terrorism incidents before they occur.

International collaborations in agro-terrorism prevention are of utmost importance. Sharing intelligence, best practices, and resources with international partners can strengthen our collective ability to detect and respond to agro-terrorism threats. Law enforcement should actively engage in international forums, exchange information, and participate in joint exercises to enhance our preparedness.

Public awareness and education on agro-terrorism threats are essential in ensuring a vigilant society. Law enforcement should actively engage with local communities, farmers, and agricultural stakeholders to raise awareness about the potential risks and encourage reporting of suspicious activities. By fostering a culture of vigilance, we can create a strong defense against agro-terrorism.

Finally, research and development of advanced detection methods for agro-terrorism are crucial. Law enforcement should support and collaborate with research institutions and technology companies to develop cutting-edge detection technologies. This includes innovative approaches like biosensors, molecular diagnostics, and artificial intelligence, which can significantly enhance our ability to detect agro-terrorism threats.

In conclusion, early detection and rapid response are critical components in protecting America's harvest from agro-terrorism. By implementing robust biosecurity measures, ensuring food supply chain security, utilizing advanced surveillance technologies, establishing emergency response protocols, conducting risk assessments, fostering international collaborations, promoting public awareness, and investing in research and development, law enforcement can effectively safeguard the nation's agricultural infrastructure and prevent agro-terrorism incidents.

Types of Surveillance and Monitoring Systems

In order to effectively protect the United States against agro-terrorism, law enforcement agencies must be equipped with advanced surveillance and monitoring systems. These systems play a crucial role in detecting and preventing potential threats to the agricultural sector, ensuring the security of the food supply chain, and safeguarding the country's crop production.

One of the most common types of surveillance systems used in agro-terrorism prevention is closed-circuit television (CCTV) cameras. These cameras are strategically placed in key locations such as farms, processing plants, and transportation hubs to monitor activities and detect any suspicious behavior. CCTV footage can be continuously monitored by law enforcement personnel or analyzed using artificial intelligence algorithms to identify potential threats.

Another important surveillance system is the use of unmanned aerial vehicles (UAVs), commonly known as drones. Drones equipped with high-resolution cameras can provide aerial surveillance over large agricultural areas, allowing law enforcement agencies to quickly identify and respond to any suspicious activities. Drones can also be used in combination with thermal imaging technology to detect anomalies in crop health or identify potential unauthorized access to agricultural facilities.

In addition to visual surveillance systems, monitoring systems that utilize sensors and data analytics are becoming increasingly important in agro-terrorism prevention. These systems can include sensors that detect changes in temperature, humidity, or chemical composition, indicating the presence of harmful substances or pathogens. By collecting and analyzing data from these sensors, law enforcement agencies can identify potential threats and take appropriate actions to mitigate risks.

Furthermore, advanced monitoring systems can integrate real-time data from multiple sources, such as weather forecasts, pest control databases, and crop health monitoring tools. This holistic approach provides a comprehensive view of the agricultural landscape and enables law enforcement agencies to proactively identify vulnerabilities and implement targeted security measures.

It is worth noting that surveillance and monitoring systems should be complemented by robust emergency response protocols. In the event of an agro-terrorism incident, law enforcement agencies must have well-defined procedures in place to rapidly respond, contain the threat, and minimize the impact on the food supply chain.

Overall, the implementation of various types of surveillance and monitoring systems is crucial for law enforcement agencies involved in protecting the United States against agro-terrorism. By leveraging advanced technologies and data analytics, these systems enhance the ability to detect and prevent potential threats, ensuring the safety and security of the nation's agricultural sector.

Implementing Surveillance and Monitoring Systems

In order to effectively combat agro-terrorism and protect the agricultural sector in the United States, it is crucial for law enforcement agencies to implement robust surveillance and monitoring systems. These systems play a vital role in detecting and preventing potential threats to the food supply chain, agricultural biosecurity, and crop protection. This subchapter will delve into the importance of surveillance and monitoring systems for agro-terrorism prevention and provide insights into various technologies and strategies that law enforcement can employ.

Surveillance and monitoring systems form the backbone of any comprehensive agro-terrorism prevention program. By leveraging advanced technologies such as drones, satellite imagery, and sensor networks, law enforcement agencies can enhance their situational awareness and gain real-time insights into potential threats. These systems enable the continuous monitoring of agricultural areas, allowing for the early detection of suspicious activities, unauthorized access, or tampering with crops and livestock.

One of the key advantages of implementing surveillance and monitoring systems is the ability to quickly identify and respond to agro-terrorism incidents. By integrating these systems with emergency response protocols, law enforcement agencies can ensure a swift and coordinated response to mitigate the impact of such incidents. Additionally, surveillance systems can provide valuable evidence for investigations and help in identifying the perpetrators responsible for agro-terrorism attacks.

Furthermore, surveillance and monitoring systems enable law enforcement agencies to conduct risk assessments and develop effective risk management strategies. By analyzing data collected from these systems, agencies can identify vulnerable areas in the agricultural infrastructure and allocate resources accordingly to strengthen security measures. This proactive approach helps in preventing potential agro-terrorism threats before they materialize.

International collaborations are also crucial in the fight against agro-terrorism. Surveillance and monitoring systems can facilitate information sharing and cooperation between different countries, enabling the early detection and prevention of transnational agro-terrorism threats. By establishing partnerships and sharing best practices, law enforcement agencies can enhance their capabilities and stay ahead of emerging risks.

Public awareness and education on agro-terrorism threats are equally important. By highlighting the potential consequences of agro-terrorism attacks on the food supply chain and emphasizing the role of surveillance and monitoring systems in prevention, law enforcement agencies can foster a culture of vigilance and encourage public participation in reporting suspicious activities.

Finally, continuous research and development of advanced detection methods for agro-terrorism are essential. By investing in innovative technologies and strategies, law enforcement can stay ahead of evolving threats and continuously improve their surveillance and monitoring systems.

In conclusion, implementing surveillance and monitoring systems is crucial for law enforcement agencies in their role of protecting the United States against agro-terrorism. These systems provide real-time insights, enhance situational awareness, and enable early detection and prevention of potential threats. By integrating surveillance and monitoring systems with emergency response protocols, conducting risk assessments, collaborating internationally, and promoting public awareness, law enforcement agencies can effectively safeguard the agricultural sector from agro-terrorism. Continuous research and development also ensure that these systems remain up-to-date and effective in countering evolving threats.

Remote Sensing Technologies

In today's interconnected world, the threat of agro-terrorism looms large, making it imperative for law enforcement agencies to stay ahead of the curve in protecting America's agricultural sector. One vital tool in this fight is remote sensing technology. This subchapter explores the various remote sensing technologies that can be employed to bolster U.S. protection against agro-terrorism.

Remote sensing technologies refer to the collection of data from a distance, without direct contact with the object or area being observed. These technologies play a crucial role in agricultural biosecurity measures, food supply chain security, crop protection strategies, and surveillance and monitoring systems for agro-terrorism.

One of the primary applications of remote sensing in agro-terrorism prevention is the monitoring of agricultural lands. Satellite imagery can provide law enforcement with real-time data on crop health, enabling them to detect any anomalies that could indicate agro-terrorism activities. Additionally, aerial drones equipped with remote sensing devices can be deployed to survey vast expanses of farmland quickly and efficiently, enhancing surveillance capabilities.

Another critical aspect of remote sensing in agro-terrorism prevention is the identification of potential vulnerabilities in agricultural infrastructure. By employing hyperspectral imaging and thermal cameras, law enforcement can identify weak points such as compromised fences or unauthorized entry into sensitive areas. This data can then be used to develop emergency response protocols to mitigate the impact of agro-terrorism incidents.

Collaborative efforts at the international level are also crucial in combating agro-terrorism. Remote sensing technologies can facilitate information sharing and coordination among law enforcement agencies globally. By establishing a network of remote sensing systems, countries can collectively monitor and respond to potential agro-terrorism threats, developing a robust defense against this transnational menace.

Public awareness and education are vital components of agro-terrorism prevention. Remote sensing technologies can be leveraged to disseminate information to the public about the risks of agro-terrorism and the importance of reporting any suspicious activities. By employing remote sensing technologies in public education campaigns, law enforcement can enhance public understanding and cooperation in safeguarding the agricultural sector.

To stay ahead of ever-evolving threats, ongoing research and development of advanced detection methods for agro-terrorism are essential. Remote sensing technologies offer an array of possibilities for improving detection capabilities, including the use of artificial intelligence and machine learning algorithms to analyze vast amounts of data and identify patterns that may indicate agro-terrorism activities.

In conclusion, remote sensing technologies have revolutionized the fight against agro-terrorism. By harnessing the power of satellite imagery, aerial drones, hyperspectral imaging, and other remote sensing devices, law enforcement agencies can enhance surveillance, monitor agricultural lands, protect infrastructure, collaborate internationally, raise public awareness, and develop advanced detection methods. With these tools at their disposal, law enforcement plays a pivotal role in securing America's harvest and safeguarding the nation against the threat of agro-terrorism.

Unmanned Aerial Vehicles (UAVs)

In recent years, the use of Unmanned Aerial Vehicles (UAVs) has rapidly expanded across various industries, including law enforcement. These remotely piloted aircraft, commonly known as drones, offer tremendous potential in enhancing the capabilities of agencies involved in U.S. protection against agro-terrorism. This subchapter explores the applications of UAVs in agriculture biosecurity measures, food supply chain security, crop protection technologies and strategies, surveillance and monitoring systems for agro-terrorism, and emergency response protocols for agro-terrorism incidents.

One of the key advantages of using UAVs in agricultural biosecurity is their ability to provide a bird's-eye view of vast agricultural areas. Equipped with high-resolution cameras and sensors, UAVs can quickly identify potential vulnerabilities in crop production and infrastructure, allowing law enforcement agencies to proactively address any weak points. Additionally, UAVs can be employed to monitor livestock, detect plant diseases, and assess the impact of natural disasters, enabling early intervention and preventing further damage.

In terms of food supply chain security, UAVs can play a crucial role in enhancing surveillance along the entire chain, from farm to table. They can be used to monitor transportation routes, storage facilities, and processing plants, ensuring the integrity and safety of the food supply. UAVs equipped with thermal imaging cameras can identify abnormal temperature variations, indicating potential spoilage or tampering. Furthermore, UAVs can assist in the identification of unauthorized activities in restricted agricultural areas, safeguarding against potential agro-terrorism threats.

Crop protection technologies and strategies can also benefit from the use of UAVs. By providing real-time data on crop health, nutrient deficiencies, and pest infestations, UAVs help farmers make informed decisions regarding pesticide application and irrigation. This targeted approach minimizes environmental impact and optimizes crop yield. UAVs can also be utilized to disperse beneficial insects or deploy precision spraying devices, reducing the need for widespread chemical treatments.

In the event of an agro-terrorism incident, UAVs can serve as invaluable tools in emergency response protocols. Equipped with thermal cameras and gas sensors, they can quickly assess the situation, identify potential hazards, and provide critical information to first responders. Additionally, UAVs can aid in the delivery of medical supplies, communication equipment, and emergency food rations to affected areas, ensuring swift and efficient response efforts.

As the field of agro-terrorism prevention continues to evolve, the use of UAVs presents exciting opportunities for law enforcement agencies. By harnessing their capabilities in surveillance, monitoring, and emergency response, agencies can enhance their ability to detect, prevent, and mitigate the impact of agro-terrorism incidents. Continued research and development of advanced detection methods and public awareness campaigns are essential in maximizing the potential of UAVs in safeguarding America's harvest. Furthermore, international collaborations in agro-terrorism prevention will foster information sharing and knowledge exchange, creating a global network of defense against this growing threat.

In conclusion, UAVs offer immense potential in U.S. protection against agro-terrorism. Their applications in agricultural biosecurity, food supply chain security, crop protection technologies, surveillance and monitoring systems, emergency response protocols, and agro-terrorism risk assessment and management are invaluable to law enforcement agencies. By embracing these technologies, agencies can strengthen their efforts in safeguarding the nation's agricultural infrastructure and ensuring a safe and secure food supply.

Data Analysis and Integration

In the fight against agro-terrorism, law enforcement agencies play a critical role in ensuring the protection of America's harvest. To effectively combat this growing threat, it is essential to employ data analysis and integration strategies that provide valuable insights and inform proactive measures.

Data analysis is crucial in identifying patterns, trends, and anomalies that may indicate potential agro-terrorism activities. By collecting and analyzing relevant data from various sources, including agricultural agencies, intelligence agencies, and law enforcement databases, valuable information can be obtained to understand the evolving nature of agro-terrorism threats.

Integration of data is equally important in establishing a comprehensive picture of the risks and vulnerabilities within the agricultural sector. By consolidating data from diverse sources, such as agricultural biosecurity measures, food supply chain security, crop protection technologies and strategies, surveillance and monitoring systems for agro-terrorism, and emergency response protocols, law enforcement can gain a holistic understanding of the potential threats and develop targeted strategies to mitigate them.

Furthermore, data integration enables law enforcement agencies to collaborate effectively with other stakeholders involved in agro-terrorism prevention. By sharing relevant information and insights with agricultural agencies, international partners, and the public, law enforcement can foster a collaborative approach that enhances the overall security of America's agricultural infrastructure.

To facilitate data analysis and integration, advanced detection methods for agro-terrorism must be developed through research and development efforts. These methods can include innovative technologies like remote sensing, geospatial analysis, and predictive modeling, which can provide valuable data for risk assessment and management.

Law enforcement agencies must also prioritize public awareness and education on agro-terrorism threats. By disseminating information regarding potential risks, preventive measures, and emergency response protocols, the public can become vigilant allies in identifying and reporting suspicious activities.

In conclusion, data analysis and integration are vital components in securing America's harvest against agro-terrorism. By harnessing the power of data, law enforcement agencies can gain valuable insights, collaborate effectively, and develop targeted strategies to prevent and respond to agro-terrorism incidents. Through international collaborations, public awareness campaigns, and research and development efforts, law enforcement can stay one step ahead of agro-terrorism threats, ensuring the safety and integrity of the nation's agricultural sector.

Chapter 7: Emergency Response Protocols for Agro-Terrorism Incidents

Establishing Emergency Response Plans

In the face of emerging threats and the increasing vulnerability of the agricultural sector, law enforcement agencies play a critical role in safeguarding the United States against agro-terrorism. One of the key components of a comprehensive approach to U.S. protection against agro-terrorism is the establishment of robust emergency response plans. These plans are essential to effectively mitigate and respond to agro-terrorism incidents, ensuring the safety and security of our nation's food supply chain.

Emergency response plans for agro-terrorism incidents must be carefully designed to address the unique challenges posed by attacks on our agricultural infrastructure. Such attacks can have a devastating impact on our economy, public health, and national security. Therefore, law enforcement agencies must collaborate with agricultural stakeholders, including farmers, food producers, and industry experts, to develop comprehensive response protocols tailored to agro-terrorism scenarios.

The first step in establishing emergency response plans is conducting a thorough agro-terrorism risk assessment. This assessment should evaluate vulnerabilities in the food supply chain, agricultural infrastructure, and crop protection technologies and strategies. By identifying potential targets and vulnerabilities, law enforcement agencies can prioritize their efforts and allocate resources effectively.

Once the risk assessment is complete, law enforcement agencies should work closely with other agencies and international collaborators to develop protocols for surveillance and monitoring systems specific to agro-terrorism. These systems enable the early detection of suspicious activities and provide crucial intelligence for preventive measures. Advanced detection methods, developed through research and development, should also be integrated into these systems to enhance their effectiveness.

Emergency response protocols should include strategies for rapid containment, quarantine, and decontamination in the event of an agro-terrorism incident. These protocols should be regularly reviewed, updated, and tested through exercises and simulations to ensure their effectiveness. Additionally, law enforcement agencies must establish clear lines of communication and coordination with other emergency response agencies, such as the fire department, emergency medical services, and public health authorities.

Public awareness and education on agro-terrorism threats are essential components of emergency response plans. Law enforcement agencies should actively engage with the public, agricultural stakeholders, and industry associations to promote vigilance and provide guidance on reporting suspicious activities. By increasing public awareness and education, we can create a strong network of eyes and ears to help prevent and respond to agro-terrorism incidents.

In conclusion, establishing emergency response plans is crucial to protecting America's harvest and ensuring the security of our food supply chain. By conducting thorough risk assessments, developing surveillance and monitoring systems, implementing effective response protocols, and fostering public awareness, law enforcement agencies can play a pivotal role in preventing and mitigating the devastating impact of agro-terrorism. Collaboration with international partners, research and development of advanced detection methods, and continuous evaluation and improvement of emergency response plans are key to staying one step ahead of evolving threats.

Incident Command System (ICS)

In any emergency situation, the ability to effectively manage and coordinate a response is crucial. This is especially true when it comes to incidents of agro-terrorism, where the potential for widespread damage and disruption to the agricultural sector is significant. The Incident Command System (ICS) is a proven framework that enables law enforcement and other agencies to effectively respond to agro-terrorism incidents and mitigate their impact on the U.S. food supply chain.

ICS is a standardized approach that provides a clear organizational structure, roles, and responsibilities to all involved parties during an emergency. It ensures a coordinated response by establishing a clear chain of command, facilitating communication, and promoting efficient resource allocation. For law enforcement agencies tasked with protecting the U.S. against agro-terrorism, understanding and implementing ICS is essential.

At its core, ICS operates on the principles of unity of command, chain of command, and span of control. This means that there is a clear hierarchy of leadership, with one Incident Commander overseeing the entire operation. This individual is responsible for making strategic decisions and coordinating efforts between various agencies involved in the response.

Underneath the Incident Commander, there are several functional areas, each with its own designated leader. These include Operations, Planning, Logistics, Finance, and Administration. Each functional area plays a crucial role in the response effort, and their leaders work closely with the Incident Commander to ensure a smooth and effective operation.

One of the key benefits of ICS is its flexibility and scalability. It can be adapted to incidents of any size or complexity, allowing for a seamless transition from routine operations to emergency response. Additionally, ICS emphasizes the importance of interagency cooperation and collaboration, ensuring that all relevant stakeholders are involved in the decision-making process.

Law enforcement agencies involved in protecting the U.S. against agro-terrorism incidents should familiarize themselves with ICS and incorporate its principles into their emergency response protocols. By doing so, they can enhance their ability to effectively manage and coordinate a response, minimize the impact of agro-terrorism incidents on the U.S. agricultural sector, and safeguard the nation's food supply chain.

To further strengthen the effectiveness of ICS in addressing agro-terrorism, ongoing research and development of advanced detection methods should be prioritized. This will enable law enforcement agencies to detect potential agro-terrorism threats at an early stage and respond swiftly and effectively. International collaborations in agro-terrorism prevention and sharing best practices will also strengthen the overall response to agro-terrorism incidents.

Moreover, public awareness and education on agro-terrorism threats should be a priority. By raising awareness among the general public and agricultural stakeholders, everyone can play a role in reporting suspicious activities and taking preventive measures to protect the U.S. agricultural infrastructure.

In conclusion, the Incident Command System is a crucial tool for law enforcement agencies engaged in protecting the U.S. against agro-terrorism incidents. By implementing ICS, agencies can ensure efficient coordination, effective resource allocation, and a swift response to mitigate the impact of agro-terrorism on the nation's food supply chain. Continued research and development, international collaborations, and public awareness are all essential components of a comprehensive approach to agro-terrorism prevention and response.

Roles and Responsibilities of Law Enforcement in Emergency Response

In the face of increasing threats to the United States' agricultural sector, law enforcement plays a critical role in the emergency response to agro-terrorism incidents. With the aim of ensuring the protection of the nation's food supply chain and agricultural biosecurity, law enforcement agencies are tasked with a wide range of responsibilities and must collaborate with various stakeholders to effectively mitigate and respond to agro-terrorism risks.

One of the primary responsibilities of law enforcement in emergency response is the development and implementation of effective surveillance and monitoring systems for agro-terrorism. By closely monitoring potential threats and suspicious activities, law enforcement agencies can detect early warning signs and prevent potential attacks. These systems may include the use of advanced technologies, such as drones and satellite imagery, to enhance surveillance capabilities and enable quick response to any suspicious activities.

Law enforcement agencies are also responsible for the development and implementation of emergency response protocols specific to agro-terrorism incidents. This includes establishing coordination mechanisms with other relevant agencies, such as agricultural and public health departments, to ensure a swift and coordinated response during emergencies. Additionally, law enforcement must ensure that personnel are trained in emergency response procedures and have access to adequate resources, equipment, and training to effectively address agro-terrorism incidents.

Agro-terrorism risk assessment and management is another crucial responsibility of law enforcement. By conducting thorough risk assessments and identifying vulnerabilities in the agricultural infrastructure, law enforcement agencies can develop targeted strategies and preventive measures to mitigate potential threats. This may involve collaborating with research institutions and industry experts to stay updated on emerging crop protection technologies and strategies.

Furthermore, law enforcement plays a vital role in protecting the agricultural infrastructure from potential agro-terrorism attacks. This includes securing critical facilities, such as food processing plants, storage facilities, and transportation hubs, to ensure the integrity of the food supply chain. Law enforcement agencies must also collaborate with international partners to share information, intelligence, and best practices in agro-terrorism prevention.

Public awareness and education on agro-terrorism threats are essential to the overall success of prevention efforts. Law enforcement agencies can actively engage with the public through community outreach programs, workshops, and educational campaigns to raise awareness about the potential risks associated with agro-terrorism. By empowering citizens with knowledge, law enforcement can foster a collective sense of responsibility and encourage the reporting of suspicious activities.

Lastly, law enforcement agencies must allocate resources for research and development of advanced detection methods for agro-terrorism. By investing in cutting-edge technologies and collaborating with research institutions, law enforcement can enhance their capabilities to detect and respond to emerging threats effectively.

In conclusion, law enforcement agencies have a crucial role in emergency response to agro-terrorism incidents. Through effective surveillance and monitoring systems, the development of emergency response protocols, risk assessment and management, infrastructure protection, international collaborations, public awareness and education initiatives, and research and development, law enforcement can contribute significantly to the protection of the United States' agricultural sector against agro-terrorism threats.

Coordinating Response Efforts

In the face of agro-terrorism threats, coordination among law enforcement agencies and other stakeholders is crucial to effectively respond to and mitigate potential incidents. This subchapter explores the importance of coordinating response efforts in protecting America's harvest and highlights the various strategies and measures that can be implemented.

One of the key aspects of coordinating response efforts is the establishment of effective communication channels among law enforcement agencies, agricultural organizations, and other relevant stakeholders. Timely and accurate information exchange is vital for early detection and rapid response to agro-terrorism incidents. This can be achieved through the development of dedicated communication networks and platforms that facilitate real-time sharing of intelligence, updates, and threat assessments.

Another critical component of effective coordination is the development and implementation of emergency response protocols specifically tailored for agro-terrorism incidents. These protocols should outline the roles and responsibilities of different agencies and organizations, as well as the steps to be taken to ensure a swift and coordinated response. Regular training drills and exercises should be conducted to test and improve the efficiency of these protocols.

Coordinating response efforts also involves the development and adoption of agro-terrorism risk assessment and management strategies. These strategies help identify vulnerabilities in the agricultural sector, prioritize potential targets, and allocate resources accordingly. By conducting comprehensive risk assessments, law enforcement agencies can focus their efforts on high-risk areas and implement preventive measures to reduce the likelihood of agro-terrorism incidents.

Furthermore, collaboration at the international level is essential in combating agro-terrorism. Sharing best practices, intelligence, and resources with foreign counterparts can enhance the overall preparedness and response capabilities of all involved nations. Establishing partnerships and information-sharing mechanisms with international agencies and organizations can significantly strengthen the global defense against agro-terrorism.

Lastly, public awareness and education play a vital role in preventing and responding to agro-terrorism threats. Law enforcement agencies should actively engage with agricultural communities, industry stakeholders, and the general public to raise awareness about the risks posed by agro-terrorism and the importance of reporting any suspicious activities. Education campaigns can help empower individuals to identify potential threats and take appropriate action.

In conclusion, coordinating response efforts is instrumental in protecting America's harvest from agro-terrorism. By establishing effective communication channels, developing emergency response protocols, conducting risk assessments, fostering international collaborations, and promoting public awareness, law enforcement agencies can enhance their ability to detect, prevent, and respond to agro-terrorism incidents.

Collaboration between Law Enforcement and Emergency Management Agencies

Effective collaboration between law enforcement and emergency management agencies is crucial in ensuring the protection of the United States against agro-terrorism. The threat of agro-terrorism, which involves deliberate attacks on agricultural systems, poses significant risks to food supply chain security and agricultural biosecurity measures. In order to effectively address these threats, it is essential for law enforcement and emergency management agencies to work together seamlessly.

One key aspect of collaboration between these agencies is the sharing of information and intelligence. Law enforcement agencies possess valuable intelligence regarding potential agro-terrorism threats, while emergency management agencies have expertise in responding to and managing emergencies. By sharing information and intelligence, these agencies can enhance their understanding of potential threats and develop appropriate response protocols.

Surveillance and monitoring systems are vital tools in detecting and preventing agro-terrorism incidents. Law enforcement agencies play a vital role in the deployment and maintenance of these systems, while emergency management agencies utilize the collected data to assess risks and develop response plans. Collaborative efforts in the development and implementation of surveillance and monitoring systems can significantly enhance the detection and prevention of agro-terrorism incidents.

In the event of an agro-terrorism incident, effective emergency response protocols are essential to minimize the impact and protect public safety. Law enforcement agencies and emergency management agencies must work closely to develop and rehearse these protocols. By conducting joint training exercises and simulations, these agencies can improve their coordination and response capabilities, ensuring a swift and effective response to agro-terrorism incidents.

Agro-terrorism risk assessment and management is another critical area where collaboration between law enforcement and emergency management agencies is essential. By conducting comprehensive risk assessments and developing robust risk management strategies, these agencies can proactively address potential vulnerabilities in agricultural infrastructure. Collaboration in this area ensures that all potential risks are identified and mitigated effectively.

Furthermore, international collaborations in agro-terrorism prevention are crucial in a globalized world. Law enforcement and emergency management agencies must collaborate with international partners to share best practices, exchange intelligence, and develop joint response strategies. Close cooperation with international agencies and organizations enhances the collective ability to detect and prevent agro-terrorism incidents.

Public awareness and education on agro-terrorism threats are essential in fostering a vigilant society. Law enforcement and emergency management agencies should work together to develop educational campaigns and outreach programs to raise awareness among the public, agricultural sector, and relevant stakeholders. By educating the public about the risks of agro-terrorism and promoting reporting mechanisms, the chances of preventing and detecting potential threats are significantly increased.

Finally, research and development of advanced detection methods for agro-terrorism are paramount. Collaborative efforts between law enforcement and emergency management agencies, as well as academia and industry, can drive innovation in this field. By investing in research and development, agencies can stay ahead of emerging agro-terrorism threats and develop cutting-edge technologies and strategies to counter them.

In conclusion, collaboration between law enforcement and emergency management agencies is essential in securing America's harvest against agro-terrorism. Through information sharing, development of surveillance systems, joint training, risk assessment and management, international collaborations, public awareness, and research and development, these agencies can enhance their capabilities to detect, prevent, and respond to agro-terrorism incidents. Working together, law enforcement and emergency management agencies can safeguard the agricultural sector and protect the nation's food supply chain from agro-terrorism threats.

Communicating with the Public and Media during Agro-Terrorism Incidents

In the face of agro-terrorism incidents, effective communication with the public and media is crucial for maintaining public trust, minimizing panic, and ensuring the successful management of the situation. Law enforcement plays a pivotal role in disseminating accurate and timely information to the public, keeping them informed and educated about the threats and actions being taken to protect against agro-terrorism. This subchapter will delve into the strategies and best practices for communicating with the public and media during agro-terrorism incidents.

One of the key aspects to consider when communicating with the public and media is to establish a clear and consistent message. It is important to convey accurate information without causing unnecessary alarm. Law enforcement agencies should work closely with agricultural authorities and experts to ensure that the information shared is reliable, up-to-date, and easy to understand.

Another essential element is the use of multiple communication channels. Utilizing both traditional and digital platforms will help reach a wider audience. Press conferences, press releases, social media, and websites can be used to provide updates, share safety measures, and address concerns. Additionally, law enforcement should coordinate with local news outlets to ensure that accurate information is being reported.

During agro-terrorism incidents, it is crucial to be transparent and responsive to public inquiries. Establishing a designated spokesperson or communication team can help streamline the flow of information and ensure consistency in messaging. This team should be trained in crisis communication techniques and be prepared to address a range of questions and concerns from the public and media.

Public education and awareness play a significant role in preventing agro-terrorism incidents. Law enforcement agencies should proactively engage in public outreach campaigns, educating citizens about the threats of agro-terrorism and the measures being taken to mitigate them. This can be done through workshops, community meetings, and collaborations with agricultural organizations and educational institutions.

Furthermore, international collaborations in agro-terrorism prevention should be emphasized. Sharing information and resources with other countries can help strengthen global agricultural biosecurity measures and enhance the collective ability to detect, prevent, and respond to agro-terrorism incidents.

Lastly, research and development of advanced detection methods for agro-terrorism should be encouraged. By investing in innovative technologies and strategies, law enforcement can stay ahead of evolving threats and effectively safeguard the agricultural sector.

In conclusion, effective communication with the public and media is vital during agro-terrorism incidents. Law enforcement agencies must prioritize clear and consistent messaging, utilize multiple communication channels, be transparent and responsive, engage in public education and awareness campaigns, and foster international collaborations. By following these strategies, law enforcement can enhance public trust, mitigate panic, and effectively protect against agro-terrorism.

Chapter 8: Agro-Terrorism Risk Assessment and Management

Conducting Risk Assessments

In the fight against agro-terrorism, law enforcement plays a crucial role in ensuring the protection of America's harvest and securing the nation's food supply chain. One of the key tools in this battle is conducting risk assessments, which allow law enforcement agencies to identify potential vulnerabilities and develop effective strategies to mitigate agro-terrorism threats.

Risk assessments involve a systematic evaluation of various factors that could make agricultural infrastructure susceptible to agro-terrorism attacks. This includes analyzing the vulnerabilities of crop production, processing facilities, transportation networks, and storage facilities. By identifying these vulnerabilities, law enforcement can prioritize their efforts and allocate resources to areas that are most at risk.

Agricultural biosecurity measures are an important component of risk assessments. This involves implementing measures such as strict access controls, biosecurity training for farmers and agricultural workers, and the use of surveillance and monitoring systems to detect any suspicious activities. Law enforcement must work closely with agricultural stakeholders to develop and implement these measures, ensuring that they are practical, cost-effective, and in compliance with legal and ethical standards.

The risk assessments should also address the potential impact of agro-terrorism on the food supply chain. This includes evaluating the vulnerability of transportation systems, storage facilities, and distribution networks. By identifying potential weak points in the food supply chain, law enforcement can develop strategies to enhance security and prevent any disruptions that could have severe consequences for public health and safety.

Crop protection technologies and strategies are another important aspect of risk assessments. Law enforcement agencies need to stay updated on the latest advancements in crop protection methods to effectively combat agro-terrorism. This includes researching and developing advanced detection methods, such as sensors and drones, to identify potential threats early on.

Emergency response protocols are a critical part of risk assessments. Law enforcement agencies must establish clear protocols for responding to agro-terrorism incidents, including coordination with other agencies and stakeholders. This ensures a swift and effective response to mitigate the impact of an attack and prevent further harm.

International collaborations are also essential in agro-terrorism prevention. Risk assessments should include an evaluation of international partnerships and cooperation, as agro-terrorism is a global threat that requires a unified response. Sharing information, intelligence, and best practices with international partners can significantly enhance the prevention and detection of agro-terrorism activities.

Public awareness and education on agro-terrorism threats are vital for risk assessments. Law enforcement agencies should work with the public, farmers, and agricultural workers to raise awareness about the risks of agro-terrorism and the importance of reporting any suspicious activities. This can help create a vigilant community that actively participates in the protection of the nation's agricultural infrastructure.

In conclusion, conducting risk assessments is crucial for law enforcement agencies in their efforts to protect America's harvest and secure the nation against agro-terrorism. By identifying vulnerabilities, implementing biosecurity measures, enhancing crop protection technologies, establishing emergency response protocols, fostering international collaborations, and raising public awareness, law enforcement can effectively manage and mitigate the risks posed by agro-terrorism.

Identifying Vulnerabilities and Threats

In the fight against agro-terrorism, it is crucial for law enforcement agencies to be equipped with the knowledge and tools to identify vulnerabilities and threats within the agricultural sector. This subchapter aims to provide a comprehensive understanding of the various aspects that need to be considered to ensure U.S. protection against agro-terrorism.

One of the key areas that law enforcement professionals need to focus on is agricultural biosecurity measures. By carefully analyzing the vulnerabilities in the agricultural system, law enforcement can develop strategies and protocols to prevent and respond to potential threats. This includes securing farms, livestock, and agricultural facilities, as well as implementing strict biosecurity protocols to minimize the risk of biological attacks on crops and livestock.

Additionally, law enforcement should collaborate with experts in the field to enhance food supply chain security. This involves identifying weak points in the supply chain, such as transportation routes and storage facilities, and implementing robust security measures to mitigate the risk of agro-terrorism incidents. By working closely with stakeholders in the food industry, law enforcement can ensure that the entire supply chain is protected from potential threats.

The use of advanced crop protection technologies and strategies is another crucial aspect to consider. Law enforcement should familiarize themselves with cutting-edge technologies that can help detect and prevent agro-terrorism incidents. This may include the use of drones, satellite imagery, and other surveillance and monitoring systems to enhance situational awareness and detect any suspicious activities in agricultural areas.

Emergency response protocols for agro-terrorism incidents are also essential. Law enforcement agencies must establish clear guidelines and procedures to handle potential threats swiftly and effectively. This includes coordinating with other agencies, such as fire departments and emergency medical services, to ensure a coordinated response and minimize the impact of agro-terrorism incidents.

Furthermore, law enforcement professionals should engage in agro-terrorism risk assessment and management. By conducting thorough risk assessments, they can identify vulnerabilities, evaluate potential threats, and develop strategies to mitigate risks. This requires a comprehensive understanding of the agricultural infrastructure and the potential consequences of an agro-terrorism attack.

International collaborations in agro-terrorism prevention are vital in today's interconnected world. Law enforcement agencies should actively engage with their counterparts in other countries to share information, intelligence, and best practices. By working together, they can strengthen their collective ability to prevent and respond to agro-terrorism incidents.

Lastly, public awareness and education on agro-terrorism threats play a crucial role in preventing such incidents. Law enforcement professionals should actively engage with the public, farmers, and other stakeholders to raise awareness about the risks and potential consequences of agro-terrorism. This can be achieved through outreach programs, workshops, and educational campaigns.

To support these efforts, research and development of advanced detection methods for agro-terrorism should be prioritized. Law enforcement agencies should collaborate with researchers and scientists to develop innovative technologies and techniques that can detect and prevent agro-terrorism incidents more effectively.

In conclusion, identifying vulnerabilities and threats is a critical component of law enforcement's role in U.S. protection against agro-terrorism. By focusing on areas such as agricultural biosecurity measures, food supply chain security, crop protection technologies and strategies, surveillance and monitoring systems, emergency response protocols, risk assessment and management, agricultural infrastructure protection, international collaborations, public awareness and education, and advanced detection methods, law enforcement can strengthen their ability to prevent and respond to agro-terrorism incidents.

Assessing Consequences and Impact

In the realm of U.S. Protection Against Agro-Terrorism, it is crucial for law enforcement professionals to understand the potential consequences and impact of such incidents. Assessing these factors allows for effective planning and response strategies, ensuring the safeguarding of our nation's agricultural sector and food supply chain. This subchapter delves into the various aspects related to assessing consequences and impact in agro-terrorism incidents.

One of the primary concerns in agro-terrorism is the potential devastation it can cause to the agricultural industry. Attacks targeting crops, livestock, or the food supply chain can have severe economic, social, and public health consequences. Understanding the magnitude of these impacts is essential for law enforcement to grasp the gravity of the situation and allocate resources accordingly.

Agricultural biosecurity measures play a crucial role in preventing and mitigating agro-terrorism incidents. Assessing the consequences of a breach in these measures helps law enforcement identify vulnerabilities and implement necessary safeguards. By understanding the potential impact of specific biosecurity breaches, law enforcement can better prioritize their efforts and allocate resources to areas that require immediate attention.

Another crucial aspect is the assessment of existing crop protection technologies and strategies. Law enforcement professionals need to stay up to date with the latest advancements in this field to effectively counter agro-terrorism threats. By assessing the consequences of potential attacks on crops and evaluating the efficacy of existing protection methods, law enforcement agencies can develop proactive strategies to deter and respond to agro-terrorism incidents.

Surveillance and monitoring systems also play a pivotal role in agro-terrorism prevention. Understanding the potential consequences of surveillance system failures or vulnerabilities can help law enforcement identify areas for improvement. Additionally, assessing the impact of enhanced monitoring can aid in identifying potential threats and swiftly responding to suspicious activities.

Emergency response protocols are vital in minimizing the impact of agro-terrorism incidents. By assessing the potential consequences of different scenarios, law enforcement can develop comprehensive response plans. These plans should include coordination with relevant agencies, rapid deployment of resources, and effective communication strategies to minimize the impact on public health and safety.

Furthermore, law enforcement professionals must conduct comprehensive agro-terrorism risk assessments and develop management strategies accordingly. Assessing the potential consequences of different attack scenarios helps prioritize preventive measures and allocate resources effectively.

International collaborations in agro-terrorism prevention are crucial to combating this global threat. By understanding the consequences and impact of agro-terrorism incidents in other countries, law enforcement agencies can learn from best practices and develop effective prevention strategies.

Public awareness and education play a vital role in agro-terrorism prevention. Assessing the potential consequences of agro-terrorism incidents helps law enforcement professionals communicate the severity of the threat to the public. This awareness encourages individuals to report suspicious activities and enhances overall preparedness.

Finally, ongoing research and development of advanced detection methods for agro-terrorism are paramount. By assessing the potential impact of new detection technologies, law enforcement can stay ahead of agro-terrorism threats and effectively protect the agricultural sector.

In conclusion, assessing consequences and impact is a critical component of law enforcement's role in U.S. Protection Against Agro-Terrorism. By understanding the potential consequences of attacks, vulnerabilities in biosecurity measures, and the impact on the agricultural industry, law enforcement professionals can develop proactive strategies, enhance surveillance and monitoring systems, and effectively respond to agro-terrorism incidents. Collaboration, public awareness, and ongoing research are essential in this collective effort to secure America's harvest.

Risk Management Strategies

Effective risk management is an essential component in safeguarding the United States against the ever-looming threat of agro-terrorism.

As law enforcement professionals involved in U.S. protection against agro-terrorism, it is imperative to have a comprehensive understanding of risk management strategies to effectively mitigate and respond to potential incidents. This subchapter will explore various risk management strategies that can be employed to protect the nation's agricultural sector and ensure food supply chain security.

One of the primary strategies in risk management is the implementation of robust agricultural biosecurity measures. These measures encompass a range of preventive actions, such as controlling access to sensitive areas, implementing strict biosecurity protocols, and enhancing the security of agricultural facilities. By establishing these measures, law enforcement agencies can minimize the risk of unauthorized access and the introduction of harmful agents into the food system.

Furthermore, it is crucial to adopt crop protection technologies and strategies that can detect and prevent agro-terrorism incidents. These technologies include advanced surveillance and monitoring systems that can detect unusual activities, unauthorized movements, or deviations from normal patterns. By investing in these technologies, law enforcement agencies can enhance their situational awareness and respond promptly to potential threats.

In addition to preventive measures, it is essential to develop emergency response protocols specifically tailored for agro-terrorism incidents. These protocols should include coordination mechanisms among law enforcement agencies, agricultural stakeholders, and emergency response teams. By establishing clear lines of communication and collaboration, the response to agro-terrorism incidents can be swift, efficient, and effective.

Risk assessment is another critical aspect of risk management strategies. Law enforcement professionals should conduct thorough agro-terrorism risk assessments to identify vulnerabilities, assess potential threats, and prioritize mitigation efforts. These assessments should be regularly updated to address emerging risks and changing threat landscapes.

To ensure the protection of agricultural infrastructure, law enforcement agencies must collaborate with international partners. Sharing information, best practices, and intelligence with foreign counterparts can enhance global efforts in agro-terrorism prevention. Additionally, public awareness and education campaigns are essential to inform farmers, agricultural workers, and the general public about agro-terrorism threats, mitigation strategies, and the importance of reporting suspicious activities.

Lastly, continuous research and development of advanced detection methods for agro-terrorism are crucial in staying ahead of evolving threats. Investing in cutting-edge technologies and supporting scientific research can lead to the development of innovative detection tools that can quickly identify and neutralize potential attacks.

In conclusion, risk management strategies play a pivotal role in protecting the United States against agro-terrorism. Law enforcement professionals involved in U.S. protection against agro-terrorism must be well-versed in agricultural biosecurity measures, crop protection technologies, surveillance systems, emergency response protocols, risk assessments, infrastructure protection, international collaborations, public awareness, and advanced detection methods. By implementing these strategies, we can ensure the security and resilience of our nation's agricultural sector and maintain the integrity of our food supply chain.

Risk Mitigation Measures

In the fight against agro-terrorism, law enforcement plays a crucial role in ensuring the protection of America's harvest. By implementing effective risk mitigation measures, we can safeguard our agricultural systems and food supply chain from potential threats. This subchapter explores various strategies and technologies that can be employed to mitigate the risks associated with agro-terrorism, while addressing the specific needs and interests of law enforcement.

One of the key aspects of risk mitigation is agricultural biosecurity measures. Law enforcement agencies should collaborate with agricultural stakeholders to develop and enforce strict biosecurity protocols. These measures include controlling access to sensitive areas, implementing rigorous screening procedures for individuals and vehicles, and monitoring and tracking the movement of livestock and agricultural products. By establishing a comprehensive biosecurity framework, we can prevent unauthorized individuals from tampering with our food production systems.

Efficient food supply chain security is another critical component of risk mitigation. Law enforcement should work closely with food producers, processors, and distributors to identify vulnerabilities in the supply chain and implement robust security measures. This may involve conducting regular audits, improving traceability systems, and enhancing the physical security of storage facilities and transportation routes. By ensuring the integrity of the food supply chain, we can minimize the risk of agro-terrorism incidents.

Crop protection technologies and strategies are essential for mitigating risks related to agro-terrorism. Law enforcement agencies should collaborate with agricultural experts to develop and promote the use of advanced technologies such as drones, satellite imagery, and remote sensing to detect and respond to potential threats. Additionally, implementing integrated pest management techniques, crop diversification, and genetic resistance can help reduce the vulnerability of crops to agro-terrorism attacks.

Surveillance and monitoring systems play a crucial role in early detection and prevention of agro-terrorism incidents. Law enforcement should invest in state-of-the-art surveillance technologies, such as video analytics, sensors, and data analytics platforms, to enhance situational awareness in agricultural areas. By detecting anomalies and suspicious activities in real-time, law enforcement can respond swiftly to mitigate potential threats.

Emergency response protocols are vital for effective management of agro-terrorism incidents. Law enforcement agencies should collaborate with other relevant stakeholders to develop and regularly update emergency response plans. These plans should include procedures for rapid containment, decontamination, and investigation of agro-terrorism incidents. By conducting regular drills and training exercises, law enforcement can ensure a coordinated and efficient response during crisis situations.

Agro-terrorism risk assessment and management should be an ongoing process. Law enforcement agencies should work alongside experts to conduct comprehensive risk assessments, identify vulnerabilities, and prioritize mitigation efforts. By regularly reviewing and updating risk assessment methodologies, law enforcement can stay ahead of emerging threats and adapt their strategies accordingly.

International collaborations are essential for effective agro-terrorism prevention. Law enforcement agencies should actively participate in international forums and share best practices with counterparts from other countries. By fostering global partnerships, we can enhance information sharing, intelligence exchange, and joint operations to combat agro-terrorism threats.

Public awareness and education are critical in preventing agro-terrorism incidents. Law enforcement should engage with agricultural stakeholders and the general public to raise awareness about the potential risks and consequences of agro-terrorism. By promoting public vigilance and encouraging reporting of suspicious activities, law enforcement can create a collective defense against agro-terrorism.

Research and development of advanced detection methods are crucial for staying ahead of agro-terrorism threats. Law enforcement agencies should collaborate with research institutions and industry experts to develop cutting-edge technologies for detecting biological, chemical, and radiological agents. By investing in research and development, law enforcement can enhance their capabilities in detecting and preventing agro-terrorism incidents.

In conclusion, by implementing effective risk mitigation measures, law enforcement agencies can play a pivotal role in protecting America's harvest against agro-terrorism. From agricultural biosecurity measures to surveillance systems and emergency response protocols, law enforcement should engage in comprehensive strategies that address the specific needs of agro-terrorism prevention. Through international collaborations, public awareness, and research and development, law enforcement can ensure a resilient and secure agricultural sector for the nation.

Continuity Planning and Business Resilience

In the face of agro-terrorism threats, law enforcement plays a crucial role in ensuring the protection of America's harvest. One essential aspect of this role is developing and implementing continuity planning and business resilience strategies. These strategies are aimed at safeguarding agricultural biosecurity measures, food supply chain security, and crop protection technologies and strategies.

Continuity planning involves identifying potential vulnerabilities in the agricultural sector and developing strategies to mitigate risks. It ensures that essential functions and operations can continue in the event of an agro-terrorism incident, minimizing the impact on food production and distribution. By conducting a comprehensive risk assessment, law enforcement agencies can identify critical areas within the agricultural infrastructure that require protection.

Business resilience, on the other hand, focuses on enhancing the ability of agricultural businesses to withstand and recover from agro-terrorism incidents. This includes implementing surveillance and monitoring systems for agro-terrorism to detect and respond promptly to any threats. By investing in advanced detection methods, law enforcement can enhance their ability to identify potential agro-terrorism activities before they cause significant harm.

Furthermore, law enforcement agencies need to establish emergency response protocols specifically tailored to agro-terrorism incidents. These protocols should outline the roles and responsibilities of each stakeholder involved, including law enforcement, agricultural entities, and government agencies. By conducting regular drills and exercises, the effectiveness of these protocols can be tested, ensuring a coordinated response in the event of an agro-terrorism incident.

To enhance agricultural infrastructure protection, law enforcement agencies should collaborate with international partners. Sharing intelligence and best practices can help identify emerging threats and develop effective prevention and response strategies. Additionally, public awareness and education campaigns are essential in informing farmers, ranchers, and other stakeholders about the risks of agro-terrorism and the importance of implementing security measures.

Research and development of advanced detection methods for agro-terrorism should also be a priority. This includes investing in technologies such as remote sensing, data analytics, and biotechnology to detect and prevent potential threats. By staying at the forefront of scientific advancements, law enforcement can proactively address emerging agro-terrorism risks.

In conclusion, continuity planning and business resilience are critical components of law enforcement's role in protecting America's harvest against agro-terrorism. By implementing these strategies, law enforcement agencies can ensure the agricultural sector's ability to withstand and recover from potential threats. Collaboration with international partners, public awareness campaigns, and advanced research and development are essential in enhancing the effectiveness of these measures.

Chapter 9: Agricultural Infrastructure Protection

Protecting Critical Agricultural Infrastructure

Agricultural infrastructure plays a vital role in ensuring the stability and security of the nation's food supply chain. As the threat of agro-terrorism looms large, it becomes imperative for law enforcement agencies to take proactive measures to safeguard these critical assets. This subchapter delves into the various strategies and technologies that can be employed to protect agricultural infrastructure from potential acts of sabotage and agro-terrorism.

First and foremost, law enforcement agencies must collaborate closely with agricultural stakeholders to develop comprehensive agro-terrorism risk assessment and management plans. These plans should identify the vulnerabilities within the agricultural infrastructure and prioritize the implementation of protective measures. By conducting thorough risk assessments, law enforcement can gain insights into potential weak points that can be exploited by agro-terrorists and take appropriate actions to address them.

One key aspect of protecting critical agricultural infrastructure is the deployment of advanced surveillance and monitoring systems. These systems can include technologies such as drones, CCTV cameras, and remote sensing devices to enhance situational awareness and detect any suspicious activities. By establishing a robust surveillance network, law enforcement can rapidly identify and respond to potential agro-terrorism threats.

Emergency response protocols for agro-terrorism incidents also form a crucial part of protecting agricultural infrastructure. Law enforcement agencies must work in close coordination with other relevant stakeholders, including emergency management agencies, agricultural organizations, and local communities, to develop effective response plans. These plans should outline clear procedures for containment, evacuation, and recovery in the event of an agro-terrorism incident.

Additionally, it is essential to focus on research and development efforts to enhance the detection methods for agro-terrorism. Investing in cutting-edge technologies and innovative crop protection strategies can aid in early detection and prevention of potential threats. Law enforcement agencies should collaborate with research institutions and industry experts to stay updated with the latest advancements in agricultural biosecurity measures.

International collaborations also play a crucial role in preventing agro-terrorism. By sharing intelligence, best practices, and expertise with other countries, law enforcement agencies can strengthen the global defense against agro-terrorism threats. This collaboration can help identify potential threats at their source and prevent their spread across borders.

Lastly, public awareness and education initiatives are vital in ensuring the involvement of the broader community in agro-terrorism prevention. Law enforcement agencies should actively engage with farmers, agricultural workers, and the general public to educate them about the potential risks and the importance of reporting any suspicious activities. By fostering a culture of vigilance, law enforcement can create a strong network of eyes and ears, enhancing the overall security of agricultural infrastructure.

In conclusion, protecting critical agricultural infrastructure requires a multi-faceted approach involving risk assessment, surveillance systems, emergency response protocols, research and development, international collaborations, and public awareness. By implementing these strategies and leveraging advanced technologies, law enforcement agencies can effectively safeguard the nation's food supply chain and mitigate the risks posed by agro-terrorism.

Storage Facilities and Grain Silos

Storage facilities and grain silos play a critical role in the agricultural industry, serving as key elements of the food supply chain and ensuring the safe storage of grain and other commodities. However, these facilities also pose potential vulnerabilities to agro-terrorism, making it essential for law enforcement to understand and address these risks.

One of the primary concerns with storage facilities and grain silos is the potential for contamination or tampering of stored grain. Agro-terrorists may seek to introduce harmful substances, such as toxins or pathogens, into the grain supply, which could have devastating consequences for public health and the economy. Therefore, it is crucial for law enforcement to work closely with agricultural stakeholders to implement robust security measures and protocols.

Agricultural biosecurity measures are an integral part of protecting storage facilities and grain silos against agro-terrorism. Law enforcement should collaborate with farmers, grain handlers, and storage facility operators to develop and implement best practices for preventing unauthorized access and ensuring the integrity of stored grain. This may involve measures such as restricted access areas, surveillance cameras, and regular inspections to detect any signs of tampering or contamination.

Moreover, law enforcement should work with agricultural stakeholders to enhance the security of the physical infrastructure of storage facilities and grain silos. This includes assessing vulnerabilities, implementing protective measures, and conducting regular drills and exercises to test emergency response protocols. By establishing strong partnerships with the agricultural community, law enforcement can improve overall preparedness and response capabilities in the event of an agro-terrorism incident.

Additionally, surveillance and monitoring systems play a crucial role in detecting and preventing agro-terrorism threats. Law enforcement should encourage the use of advanced technologies, such as remote sensing, drones, and sensor networks, to enhance surveillance capabilities and quickly identify any suspicious activities near storage facilities and grain silos. These technologies can also aid in the rapid response to potential threats, minimizing the impact on the food supply chain.

International collaborations are also vital in preventing agro-terrorism. Law enforcement agencies should foster partnerships with international counterparts to share information, best practices, and intelligence on emerging agro-terrorism threats. By working together, countries can strengthen their collective ability to detect, prevent, and respond to agro-terrorism incidents.

Lastly, public awareness and education are essential in mitigating agro-terrorism risks. Law enforcement should engage with the public, agricultural stakeholders, and educational institutions to raise awareness about the potential threats, encourage reporting of suspicious activities, and promote the adoption of security measures. Furthermore, continued research and development of advanced detection methods for agro-terrorism can further bolster the capabilities of law enforcement agencies in protecting storage facilities and grain silos.

In conclusion, securing storage facilities and grain silos against agro-terrorism requires a comprehensive and collaborative approach. Law enforcement, along with agricultural stakeholders, must prioritize agricultural biosecurity measures, enhance physical infrastructure security, utilize surveillance and monitoring systems, foster international collaborations, raise public awareness, and invest in advanced detection methods. By addressing these areas, law enforcement can play a crucial role in protecting America's harvest and ensuring the security of the nation's food supply chain.

Irrigation Systems and Water Sources

In the realm of agricultural biosecurity measures and the protection of America's harvest against agro-terrorism, it is crucial for law enforcement to understand the importance of irrigation systems and water sources. The availability of water plays a significant role in ensuring the integrity and productivity of our nation's crops. This subchapter will delve into the various aspects of irrigation systems and water sources, highlighting their significance in safeguarding the food supply chain, protecting agricultural infrastructure, and managing agro-terrorism risks.

Irrigation systems are vital for providing crops with the necessary moisture to grow and thrive. Law enforcement personnel involved in U.S. protection against agro-terrorism must be familiar with the different types of irrigation systems employed in agriculture, such as surface irrigation, sprinkler systems, and drip irrigation. Understanding these systems will enable law enforcement to recognize any potential vulnerabilities that could be exploited by agro-terrorists seeking to disrupt the food supply chain.

Moreover, law enforcement should be knowledgeable about the various water sources utilized in agriculture, including rivers, lakes, reservoirs, groundwater, and recycled water. These sources may be susceptible to contamination, making them potential targets for agro-terrorism. By understanding the vulnerabilities associated with water sources, law enforcement can work in collaboration with other agencies and stakeholders to develop surveillance and monitoring systems to detect any unauthorized access or tampering.

Emergency response protocols for agro-terrorism incidents should also address the potential disruption of irrigation systems and water sources. Law enforcement professionals should be trained to quickly identify and address any threats to these critical components of the agricultural infrastructure. Additionally, risk assessment and management strategies should encompass the protection of water sources, ensuring their security and resilience against potential agro-terrorism attacks.

International collaborations in agro-terrorism prevention are essential when it comes to sharing best practices on irrigation systems and water source protection. Law enforcement agencies can learn from their counterparts in other countries and work together to develop advanced detection methods for agro-terrorism. Research and development in this field should focus on improving the efficiency and security of irrigation systems, as well as enhancing the detection of water source contamination.

Public awareness and education on agro-terrorism threats should also include information on the importance of irrigation systems and water sources. By educating farmers, agricultural workers, and the general public, law enforcement can foster a proactive approach towards protecting these critical components of our nation's food supply chain.

In conclusion, irrigation systems and water sources play a vital role in the protection of America's harvest against agro-terrorism. Law enforcement professionals involved in U.S. protection against agro-terrorism must be well-versed in the various types of irrigation systems, water sources, and their vulnerabilities. By understanding and addressing these key components, law enforcement can contribute to the resilience and security of our nation's agricultural infrastructure.

Agricultural Research Centers and Laboratories

Agricultural research centers and laboratories play a crucial role in protecting the United States against agro-terrorism, ensuring the safety and security of our nation's food supply chain. These centers and laboratories are at the forefront of agricultural biosecurity measures, crop protection technologies and strategies, and the development of advanced detection methods for agro-terrorism.

One of the primary objectives of these research centers is to conduct extensive surveillance and monitoring systems for agro-terrorism threats. Through the use of cutting-edge technology and data analysis, these centers are able to identify potential risks and vulnerabilities in our agricultural infrastructure. This information allows law enforcement agencies to develop targeted strategies to prevent and respond to agro-terrorism incidents.

In the event of an agro-terrorism incident, emergency response protocols are crucial. Agricultural research centers and laboratories work closely with law enforcement agencies to develop these protocols, ensuring a swift and coordinated response to mitigate the potential damage. These protocols include rapid containment measures, decontamination procedures, and the implementation of quarantine zones to prevent the spread of agro-terrorism agents.

To effectively manage the risk of agro-terrorism, comprehensive risk assessment and management strategies are implemented. These strategies involve analyzing potential threats, evaluating vulnerabilities, and implementing preventative measures. Agricultural research centers and laboratories collaborate with law enforcement agencies to develop these risk management plans, ensuring the protection of our agricultural infrastructure and the safety of our food supply chain.

International collaborations are also vital in agro-terrorism prevention. Agricultural research centers and laboratories work closely with their counterparts in other countries to share information, best practices, and research findings. These collaborations enhance our knowledge and understanding of agro-terrorism threats, allowing for the development of more effective prevention and response strategies.

Public awareness and education on agro-terrorism threats are essential to ensure the involvement and cooperation of the general public. Agricultural research centers and laboratories actively engage in public outreach programs, providing information and resources to educate individuals about the potential risks and impacts of agro-terrorism. Through these efforts, the public becomes a valuable ally in the fight against agro-terrorism.

In conclusion, agricultural research centers and laboratories are indispensable in the protection of the United States against agro-terrorism. Through their work in agricultural biosecurity, surveillance systems, emergency response protocols, risk assessment and management, international collaborations, public awareness, and advanced detection methods, they are at the forefront of ensuring the safety and security of our nation's food supply chain. Their contributions are crucial in the ongoing efforts of law enforcement agencies to combat agro-terrorism and safeguard our agricultural infrastructure.

Securing Agricultural Transportation

In the face of increasing threats to the nation's food supply, securing agricultural transportation has become a critical component of protecting against agro-terrorism. Law enforcement agencies play a crucial role in safeguarding the transportation infrastructure that connects farms, processing facilities, and distribution centers.

Agricultural biosecurity measures encompass a range of strategies aimed at preventing the introduction and spread of pests, diseases, and contaminants within the food supply chain. Law enforcement professionals must collaborate with industry stakeholders to ensure that transportation vehicles and facilities adhere to these biosecurity protocols. This includes implementing strict cleaning and disinfection procedures, enforcing proper waste disposal practices, and conducting regular inspections to identify potential vulnerabilities.

Food supply chain security relies on efficient and secure transportation networks. Law enforcement agencies must work closely with transportation companies to develop and enforce security protocols. This may involve conducting background checks on personnel, implementing access control measures at critical points in the supply chain, and utilizing advanced tracking and monitoring technologies to trace the movement of agricultural products.

Crop protection technologies and strategies play a vital role in mitigating the risk of agro-terrorism. Law enforcement agencies can collaborate with agricultural experts to develop and implement effective surveillance and monitoring systems. This may include the use of drones, satellite imagery, and sensor networks to detect and respond to potential threats. Additionally, law enforcement should promote the adoption of crop protection technologies such as genetically modified organisms (GMOs) and integrated pest management practices that enhance the resilience of agricultural systems.

In the event of an agro-terrorism incident, law enforcement agencies must have well-defined emergency response protocols in place. This includes establishing clear lines of communication and coordination with other agencies, developing evacuation and containment strategies, and training personnel on the identification and response to agro-terrorism threats. Regular drills and exercises should be conducted to test the effectiveness of these protocols and ensure a rapid and coordinated response.

Agro-terrorism risk assessment and management are essential for identifying vulnerabilities in the agricultural transportation sector. Law enforcement agencies can collaborate with experts in risk assessment to conduct comprehensive evaluations of the transportation infrastructure and develop strategies to mitigate potential threats. This may involve implementing physical security measures, such as fencing and surveillance cameras, and enhancing cybersecurity to protect against digital threats.

International collaborations in agro-terrorism prevention are crucial for addressing the global nature of this threat. Law enforcement agencies should engage in information-sharing initiatives, joint training exercises, and collaborative research to enhance our collective capabilities in protecting agricultural transportation systems.

Public awareness and education on agro-terrorism threats are vital for fostering a culture of vigilance within the agricultural community and the general public. Law enforcement agencies can play a pivotal role in disseminating information on potential threats, promoting best practices, and encouraging reporting of suspicious activities.

Lastly, research and development of advanced detection methods for agro-terrorism are essential for staying ahead of evolving threats. Law enforcement agencies should support and participate in research efforts aimed at developing innovative technologies that can detect and identify agro-terrorism agents quickly and accurately.

In conclusion, securing agricultural transportation is crucial for protecting against agro-terrorism. Law enforcement agencies have a pivotal role to play in collaborating with industry stakeholders, implementing biosecurity measures, ensuring food supply chain security, promoting crop protection technologies, developing surveillance and monitoring systems, establishing emergency response protocols, conducting risk assessments, fostering international collaborations, raising public awareness, and supporting research and development efforts. By prioritizing these areas, we can enhance our preparedness and resilience in the face of agro-terrorism threats.

Railways and Highways

The transportation sector plays a crucial role in the agricultural industry, ensuring the smooth movement of goods from farms to markets. However, this critical infrastructure is also vulnerable to agro-terrorism threats. In this subchapter, we will explore the importance of railways and highways in the context of agro-terrorism and discuss strategies to enhance their protection.

Railways and highways serve as lifelines for the agricultural sector, connecting farmers, processors, distributors, and consumers across the country. They facilitate the efficient movement of agricultural products, ensuring a steady supply of food for the nation. However, these transportation networks present attractive targets for agro-terrorists seeking to disrupt the food supply chain and instill fear in the population.

To safeguard railways and highways against agro-terrorism, law enforcement agencies must collaborate with various stakeholders, including transportation authorities, agricultural organizations, and private sector partners. This collaborative approach enables the sharing of intelligence, resources, and expertise, thereby enhancing the overall security posture.

One key aspect of protecting railways and highways is the implementation of advanced surveillance and monitoring systems. These systems can include technologies such as CCTV cameras, motion sensors, and drones, which provide real-time situational awareness and enable swift response to any suspicious activities. Additionally, leveraging data analytics and artificial intelligence can help in identifying patterns and anomalies that might indicate potential agro-terrorism threats.

Emergency response protocols are another crucial element in securing railways and highways. Law enforcement agencies need to establish clear guidelines and communication channels for responding to agro-terrorism incidents. Regular drills and training exercises should be conducted to ensure preparedness and coordination among different agencies involved in emergency response.

Agro-terrorism risk assessment and management should also be prioritized. This involves conducting thorough assessments of vulnerabilities and potential threats, and implementing appropriate mitigation measures. Additionally, investing in research and development of advanced detection methods can aid in the early identification of agro-terrorism threats, allowing for timely intervention and prevention.

International collaborations play a vital role in preventing agro-terrorism. Sharing information, best practices, and intelligence with other countries can help in identifying global trends and emerging threats. Collaborative efforts can also facilitate joint operations and investigations, ensuring a comprehensive response to agro-terrorism.

To raise public awareness and education on agro-terrorism threats, law enforcement agencies should engage with the agricultural community and the general public. This can be achieved through outreach programs, workshops, and public campaigns that highlight the importance of agricultural biosecurity, the potential consequences of agro-terrorism, and ways to report suspicious activities.

In conclusion, railways and highways are integral components of the agricultural infrastructure, and their protection against agro-terrorism is paramount. By implementing robust surveillance systems, emergency response protocols, risk assessment measures, and international collaborations, law enforcement agencies can enhance the security of these transportation networks and safeguard the nation's food supply chain. Public awareness and education initiatives further contribute to a vigilant and resilient society. Through these collective efforts, we can ensure the continued protection of America's harvest.

Ports and Border Crossings

In the fight against agro-terrorism, ports and border crossings play a critical role in protecting America's agricultural industry. These entry points serve as gateways for goods and people, making them vulnerable to the introduction of harmful pests, diseases, and agro-terrorism threats. Law enforcement agencies have a significant responsibility in securing these ports and border crossings, implementing robust agricultural biosecurity measures to safeguard the nation's food supply chain and prevent potential catastrophic consequences.

One of the key focus areas for law enforcement in U.S. protection against agro-terrorism is ensuring the security of ports and border crossings. By implementing stringent surveillance and monitoring systems, law enforcement agencies can effectively detect and intercept any suspicious activities or attempts to introduce harmful agents into the country. This requires constant vigilance and collaboration with other relevant agencies, such as customs and border protection, agricultural inspection services, and intelligence units.

Emergency response protocols for agro-terrorism incidents also need to be developed and practiced regularly at ports and border crossings. Law enforcement agencies should work closely with local, state, and federal partners to establish comprehensive emergency response plans that outline roles, responsibilities, and procedures for handling agro-terrorism threats. This includes establishing protocols for rapid detection, containment, and eradication of any potential threats, as well as communication strategies to ensure coordination and timely dissemination of information.

Agro-terrorism risk assessment and management are crucial components of protecting agricultural infrastructure at ports and border crossings. Law enforcement agencies should work in collaboration with scientific experts to conduct thorough risk assessments and develop risk management strategies. This includes identifying potential vulnerabilities, implementing preventive measures, and continuously evaluating and adapting security protocols to address emerging threats.

International collaborations in agro-terrorism prevention are also critical. Given the global nature of the agricultural industry, law enforcement agencies must establish strong partnerships with international counterparts to share intelligence, best practices, and technological advancements. Collaborative efforts can help identify and mitigate agro-terrorism threats before they reach American shores, and enhance the overall resilience of the global food supply chain.

Public awareness and education on agro-terrorism threats are essential to engage the public and foster a sense of collective responsibility. Law enforcement agencies should actively communicate with stakeholders, including farmers, agricultural businesses, and the general public, about the potential risks of agro-terrorism and the importance of reporting any suspicious activities. This can be achieved through community outreach programs, training sessions, and the dissemination of educational materials.

Research and development of advanced detection methods for agro-terrorism should be a priority for law enforcement agencies. By investing in cutting-edge technologies and strategies, such as crop protection technologies and surveillance systems, agencies can enhance their capabilities to detect and prevent agro-terrorism threats at ports and border crossings. This requires ongoing collaboration with research institutions, private sector partners, and industry experts to stay at the forefront of innovation.

In conclusion, securing ports and border crossings is of utmost importance in protecting America's agricultural industry against agro-terrorism threats. Law enforcement agencies play a vital role in implementing agricultural biosecurity measures, developing emergency response protocols, conducting risk assessments, fostering international collaborations, promoting public awareness, and investing in research and development. By prioritizing these efforts, law enforcement can effectively safeguard the nation's food supply chain and ensure the resilience of the agricultural sector against agro-terrorism.

Chapter 10: International Collaborations in Agro-Terrorism Prevention

Global Efforts and Initiatives

In the ever-evolving landscape of global security, the threat of agro-terrorism looms large, making it imperative for law enforcement agencies to collaborate and take proactive measures to protect the United States against such attacks. Recognizing the gravity of the situation, nations worldwide have come together to establish global efforts and initiatives aimed at preventing and mitigating the risks associated with agro-terrorism.

One of the key global initiatives in this regard is the establishment of international collaborations in agro-terrorism prevention. Countries around the world have realized that agro-terrorism knows no boundaries and requires a collective response. Through partnerships, information sharing, and joint exercises, nations can enhance their ability to identify and respond to potential threats. Such collaborations allow for the pooling of resources, expertise, and intelligence, thereby strengthening the overall security posture against agro-terrorism.

Another critical aspect of global efforts is the research and development of advanced detection methods for agro-terrorism. Governments, research institutions, and technology companies from different countries are working together to develop innovative technologies that can efficiently detect and identify potential threats to agricultural systems. These advanced detection methods encompass a wide range of technologies, including remote sensing, artificial intelligence, genomics, and sensor networks. By investing in research and development, countries can stay ahead of the curve in combating agro-terrorism.

Furthermore, public awareness and education on agro-terrorism threats play a vital role in global efforts. Governments and law enforcement agencies are working hand in hand to educate the public about the risks associated with agro-terrorism and the importance of reporting suspicious activities. Awareness campaigns, training programs, and community outreach initiatives are being conducted to ensure that citizens are equipped with the knowledge and resources to recognize and report potential threats promptly.

In addition to these initiatives, global efforts also focus on agro-terrorism risk assessment and management. Countries are adopting comprehensive risk assessment methodologies to evaluate vulnerabilities within their agricultural sectors. These assessments help in prioritizing protective measures, allocating resources effectively, and developing robust emergency response protocols for agro-terrorism incidents. By identifying and managing risks, nations can significantly enhance their resilience against agro-terrorism attacks.

To ensure the effectiveness of these efforts, agricultural infrastructure protection is also a priority on the global agenda. Governments are investing in securing critical agricultural infrastructure, including farms, research facilities, and food processing plants. Strengthened infrastructure protection measures, such as physical security systems, surveillance and monitoring systems, and access control measures, are being implemented to safeguard the entire food supply chain.

In conclusion, global efforts and initiatives are instrumental in combating the threat of agro-terrorism. Through international collaborations, research and development, public awareness, risk assessment, and infrastructure protection, countries can enhance their ability to prevent, detect, and respond to agro-terrorism incidents. By working together, law enforcement agencies and stakeholders involved in U.S. protection against agro-terrorism can create a safer and more secure agricultural landscape for the nation and its citizens.

Sharing Intelligence and Best Practices

In the ever-evolving landscape of agro-terrorism, law enforcement agencies play a crucial role in securing America's harvest. As guardians of national security, it is imperative for law enforcement officers to stay informed, share intelligence, and adopt best practices to protect the nation against agro-terrorism threats. This subchapter explores the importance of sharing intelligence and best practices in the field of U.S. protection against agro-terrorism.

Intelligence sharing is the lifeline of effective counterterrorism efforts. Law enforcement agencies must establish strong partnerships and collaborations to promote information exchange on agro-terrorism threats and emerging trends. By sharing intelligence, agencies can leverage shared knowledge and experience to enhance their understanding of potential vulnerabilities in the agricultural sector. This collaborative approach allows for a comprehensive and unified response to agro-terrorism incidents.

Moreover, sharing best practices is vital for law enforcement officers involved in ensuring agricultural biosecurity measures. By learning from successful strategies implemented in different regions or jurisdictions, law enforcement agencies can strengthen their own protocols and response capabilities. Best practices encompass a wide range of areas, including crop protection technologies and strategies, surveillance and monitoring systems, emergency response protocols, risk assessment and management, and agricultural infrastructure protection.

Law enforcement agencies should establish platforms for sharing best practices, such as conferences, workshops, and online forums. These platforms facilitate the exchange of knowledge and experiences among experts in the field, enabling participants to stay updated on the latest advancements in agro-terrorism prevention and response.

Furthermore, international collaborations play a significant role in addressing agro-terrorism threats. Given the interconnectedness of the global food supply chain, it is essential for law enforcement agencies to establish partnerships with international counterparts. Through these collaborations, agencies can share intelligence, coordinate response efforts, and collectively combat agro-terrorism on a global scale. International collaborations also provide opportunities for joint research and development of advanced detection methods, which are crucial in identifying and preventing agro-terrorism incidents.

Public awareness and education are other crucial aspects of agro-terrorism prevention. Law enforcement agencies should actively engage with the public to raise awareness about agro-terrorism threats and encourage reporting of suspicious activities. By educating farmers, agricultural workers, and the general public, law enforcement agencies can foster a proactive and vigilant community that actively participates in agro-terrorism prevention efforts.

In conclusion, sharing intelligence and best practices is indispensable for law enforcement agencies involved in U.S. protection against agro-terrorism. Through intelligence sharing, agencies can stay informed and develop a comprehensive understanding of agro-terrorism threats. Additionally, sharing best practices enhances response capabilities and fosters collaboration among agencies. International collaborations, public awareness, and education further strengthen the overall preparedness and resilience against agro-terrorism. By working together and constantly evolving, law enforcement agencies can effectively safeguard America's harvest and protect the nation against agro-terrorism threats.

Collaborative Research and Development

In the fight against agro-terrorism, collaboration is key. Law enforcement agencies play a crucial role in ensuring the protection of the United States against this growing threat. However, they cannot do it alone. Collaborative research and development efforts are essential in developing effective strategies and technologies to safeguard our agricultural industry and food supply chain.

One of the primary areas of focus in collaborative research and development is agricultural biosecurity measures. This involves the development of protocols and systems to prevent the introduction of harmful pathogens and pests into our agricultural systems. Through cooperation between law enforcement agencies, scientists, and industry stakeholders, we can identify vulnerabilities and develop innovative solutions to address them.

Another important aspect of collaborative research and development is the enhancement of crop protection technologies and strategies. By bringing together experts from various fields, including agriculture, biology, and law enforcement, we can develop advanced methods to protect our crops from intentional contamination. This includes the development of resistant varieties, the use of biocontrol agents, and the implementation of sustainable farming practices.

Surveillance and monitoring systems are also critical in detecting and preventing agro-terrorism incidents. Through collaborative research and development, we can develop sophisticated technologies and techniques to monitor our agricultural systems. This includes the use of drones, satellites, and sensor networks to detect and respond to potential threats in real-time.

Emergency response protocols are another crucial area that requires collaboration. By working together, law enforcement agencies can develop comprehensive protocols to respond quickly and effectively in the event of an agro-terrorism incident. This includes coordination with other agencies, such as public health departments and emergency management agencies, to ensure a swift response and minimize the impact on public safety.

Collaborative research and development efforts also encompass agro-terrorism risk assessment and management. By pooling resources and expertise, we can identify high-risk areas and develop strategies to mitigate these risks. This includes conducting vulnerability assessments, analyzing threat intelligence, and implementing proactive measures to prevent agro-terrorism incidents.

International collaborations are also vital in agro-terrorism prevention. By sharing information, best practices, and intelligence with our international partners, we can enhance our collective ability to detect and prevent potential threats. This includes cooperation in intelligence sharing, joint training exercises, and the establishment of global response networks.

Furthermore, public awareness and education play a critical role in agro-terrorism prevention. Collaborative research and development efforts can help in developing educational programs and campaigns to raise awareness about the threats posed by agro-terrorism. By engaging with the public, we can encourage vigilance and promote a sense of shared responsibility in protecting our agricultural industry and food supply chain.

Lastly, research and development of advanced detection methods are essential in combating agro-terrorism. Collaborative efforts can focus on developing innovative technologies, such as rapid diagnostic tools and advanced sensing systems, to detect and identify potential threats quickly.

In conclusion, collaborative research and development is vital in the fight against agro-terrorism. By bringing together law enforcement agencies, scientists, industry stakeholders, and international partners, we can develop effective strategies, technologies, and protocols to protect our agricultural industry and ensure the security of our food supply chain. Through cooperation and shared expertise, we can stay one step ahead of agro-terrorism threats and safeguard America's harvest.

Interagency Cooperation and Partnerships

In the fight against agro-terrorism, effective interagency cooperation and partnerships are crucial to ensuring the security and protection of America's agricultural sector. Law enforcement agencies play a significant role in this effort, working alongside various government agencies and organizations to develop a comprehensive strategy that addresses the unique challenges posed by agro-terrorism.

Collaboration between law enforcement agencies, such as local police departments, state troopers, and federal agencies like the FBI and Department of Homeland Security, is essential to effectively detect, prevent, and respond to agro-terrorism incidents. By sharing intelligence, resources, and expertise, these agencies can create a unified front against potential threats to our nation's food supply.

Furthermore, partnerships with agricultural and biosecurity agencies are vital for implementing agricultural biosecurity measures. These measures include the development and enforcement of strict protocols for pest and disease control, biosecurity training for farmers and agricultural workers, and the establishment of surveillance and monitoring systems to detect any suspicious activities or outbreaks. Through collaboration, law enforcement can work hand-in-hand with these agencies to ensure the integrity and security of the food supply chain.

Additionally, law enforcement agencies should forge alliances with crop protection technology and strategy developers to stay updated on the latest advancements in agricultural security. By staying informed about cutting-edge technologies and strategies, law enforcement can better understand the evolving nature of agro-terrorism threats and respond accordingly.

Emergency response protocols are another critical area where interagency cooperation is paramount. Law enforcement agencies must work closely with emergency responders, such as fire departments, medical services, and hazmat teams, to develop coordinated response plans for agro-terrorism incidents. These protocols should include guidelines for evacuations, decontamination procedures, and communication strategies to ensure a swift and effective response.

Agro-terrorism risk assessment and management is a complex task that requires collaboration between law enforcement and agricultural experts. By conducting comprehensive risk assessments and implementing preventive measures, such as securing agricultural infrastructure and enhancing surveillance systems, law enforcement can proactively mitigate potential vulnerabilities.

International collaborations are also crucial in agro-terrorism prevention. By working with foreign governments and organizations, law enforcement agencies can exchange information, intelligence, and best practices to address global agro-terrorism threats collectively. These partnerships can also facilitate joint training exercises and research initiatives to enhance detection methods and response capabilities.

Public awareness and education play a pivotal role in agro-terrorism prevention. Law enforcement agencies should collaborate with government agencies, educational institutions, and industry stakeholders to raise public awareness about the threats posed by agro-terrorism and the importance of reporting suspicious activities. By conducting outreach programs and disseminating educational materials, law enforcement can empower individuals to play an active role in safeguarding our nation's food supply.

Finally, research and development of advanced detection methods for agro-terrorism require close collaboration between law enforcement agencies and research institutions. By investing in research initiatives, law enforcement can stay at the forefront of technological advancements, enabling them to identify and respond to emerging agro-terrorism threats effectively.

In conclusion, interagency cooperation and partnerships are vital for law enforcement's role in protecting the United States against agro-terrorism. By working collaboratively with various stakeholders, law enforcement can strengthen our agricultural biosecurity measures, secure the food supply chain, develop advanced surveillance and monitoring systems, establish emergency response protocols, conduct risk assessments, protect agricultural infrastructure, foster international collaborations, raise public awareness, and invest in research and development. Together, these efforts form a comprehensive strategy to safeguard America's harvest from the ever-evolving threat of agro-terrorism.

International Law Enforcement Cooperation

In the globalized world we live in today, the threats we face are not limited by national borders. This is especially true when it comes to the protection against agro-terrorism, a growing concern for the United States and its agricultural sector. To effectively combat this threat, it is crucial for law enforcement agencies to engage in international cooperation and collaboration.

International law enforcement cooperation plays a vital role in the prevention and response to agro-terrorism incidents. By sharing information, intelligence, and best practices with our international partners, we can enhance our collective ability to detect, deter, and mitigate agro-terrorism risks. This collaboration is essential in safeguarding our nation's food supply chain, agricultural biosecurity measures, and crop protection technologies and strategies.

Surveillance and monitoring systems for agro-terrorism require a global perspective. Through international partnerships, we can exchange knowledge and expertise in the development and implementation of such systems. By pooling resources and sharing technological advancements, we can improve our ability to monitor and detect suspicious activities that may pose a threat to our agricultural infrastructure.

Emergency response protocols for agro-terrorism incidents must also be coordinated at an international level. By establishing clear communication channels and protocols with our global partners, we can ensure swift and effective responses to any potential agro-terrorism incidents. This collaboration includes sharing resources, training programs, and conducting joint exercises to enhance our readiness and response capabilities.

Agro-terrorism risk assessment and management is another area where international collaboration is crucial. By working together, we can identify and analyze emerging threats, assess vulnerabilities, and develop comprehensive risk management strategies. This collaboration allows us to stay ahead of evolving agro-terrorism tactics and adapt our prevention and response measures accordingly.

International collaborations also play a significant role in public awareness and education on agro-terrorism threats. By sharing information and engaging in joint public outreach campaigns, we can raise awareness among the general public, agricultural stakeholders, and law enforcement agencies about the risks and consequences of agro-terrorism. This collective effort ensures that everyone involved is prepared and vigilant against potential threats.

Lastly, research and development of advanced detection methods for agro-terrorism necessitate international cooperation. By collaborating on research initiatives, sharing data and findings, and conducting joint experiments, we can accelerate the development of cutting-edge technologies and techniques to detect and prevent agro-terrorism incidents.

In conclusion, international law enforcement cooperation is vital in the protection against agro-terrorism. By working together with our international partners, we can strengthen our collective ability to prevent, detect, and respond to agro-terrorism threats. This collaboration encompasses various aspects, including surveillance systems, emergency response protocols, risk assessment, public awareness, and research and development. Together, we can ensure the security and resilience of our agricultural sector and the protection of our nation's food supply chain.

Joint Training and Exercises

In the ongoing battle against agro-terrorism, law enforcement agencies play a crucial role in safeguarding America's harvest. To effectively combat this threat, it is imperative that these agencies engage in joint training and exercises. This subchapter delves into the significance of such collaboration, highlighting its benefits and exploring various aspects of joint training and exercises for law enforcement personnel involved in U.S. protection against agro-terrorism.

Joint training and exercises provide an opportunity for law enforcement agencies to enhance their skills, knowledge, and preparedness to respond to agro-terrorism incidents. By working together, agencies can pool their resources, expertise, and experience, creating a cohesive and coordinated response. Through joint training, law enforcement personnel can familiarize themselves with the unique challenges posed by agro-terrorism, such as agricultural biosecurity measures, food supply chain security, and crop protection technologies and strategies.

Surveillance and monitoring systems for agro-terrorism are critical components of prevention and detection. Joint training exercises can help law enforcement personnel understand these systems and practice their implementation, ensuring effective surveillance and detection of potential agro-terrorism threats. Additionally, emergency response protocols specific to agro-terrorism incidents can be developed, tested, and refined through joint exercises, enabling a swift and efficient response in the event of an attack.

Agro-terrorism risk assessment and management are vital in mitigating potential threats. Joint training allows law enforcement agencies to collaborate on risk assessment methodologies, sharing best practices and lessons learned. By jointly evaluating vulnerabilities in agricultural infrastructure and supply chains, agencies can develop targeted strategies to prevent and respond to agro-terrorism incidents effectively.

International collaborations in agro-terrorism prevention are essential, given the global nature of this threat. Joint training exercises can facilitate the exchange of knowledge, expertise, and intelligence between international law enforcement agencies, fostering cooperation and enhancing the collective ability to combat agro-terrorism on a global scale.

Public awareness and education on agro-terrorism threats are crucial in mobilizing communities and garnering support. Joint training exercises can incorporate public engagement initiatives, allowing law enforcement agencies to educate the public about the risks and consequences of agro-terrorism and the role individuals can play in prevention and reporting suspicious activities.

Furthermore, research and development of advanced detection methods for agro-terrorism require collaboration between law enforcement agencies and scientific institutions. Joint training exercises can facilitate this partnership, allowing for the testing and refinement of cutting-edge detection technologies and methodologies.

In conclusion, joint training and exercises are invaluable tools for law enforcement agencies involved in U.S. protection against agro-terrorism. By collaborating and sharing resources, knowledge, and expertise, agencies can enhance their preparedness, response capabilities, and risk management strategies. Through joint training, law enforcement personnel can effectively address the unique challenges posed by agro-terrorism, ensuring the security of America's harvest and preserving national food supply chains.

Chapter 11: Public Awareness and Education on Agro-Terrorism Threats

Importance of Public Awareness

Public awareness is a critical component in the protection against agro-terrorism, and it plays a vital role in safeguarding America's harvest. As law enforcement officials tasked with securing the nation's agricultural biosecurity and ensuring food supply chain security, it is imperative to recognize the significance of public awareness in this endeavor.

Agricultural biosecurity measures are only effective when the public understands the importance of their role in preventing agro-terrorism. By raising public awareness, law enforcement can educate citizens about the potential threats to our agricultural infrastructure and the devastating consequences that agro-terrorism can have on our economy, public health, and national security.

Through targeted outreach programs, law enforcement can inform the public about the various crop protection technologies and strategies employed to mitigate agro-terrorism risks. This knowledge empowers citizens, farmers, and other stakeholders to actively participate in implementing these measures and report any suspicious activities that may pose a threat to our food supply.

Surveillance and monitoring systems for agro-terrorism depend on public cooperation. By educating the public about the signs of agro-terrorism and encouraging them to report any unusual activities, law enforcement can create a network of vigilant citizens who serve as an extra set of eyes in identifying potential threats. This collaborative approach enhances the effectiveness of surveillance efforts, enabling early detection and swift response to agro-terrorism incidents.

Emergency response protocols for agro-terrorism incidents rely on a well-informed public. By disseminating information on emergency procedures and protocols, law enforcement can ensure that citizens know how to respond in case of an agro-terrorism attack. This knowledge not only saves lives but also minimizes the potential damage to agricultural assets and helps restore normalcy swiftly.

Agro-terrorism risk assessment and management are enhanced through public awareness campaigns. By educating the public about the vulnerabilities in our agricultural infrastructure and the potential consequences of an attack, law enforcement can foster a culture of preparedness and resilience. This proactive approach helps identify and address vulnerabilities, ensuring a safer and more secure agricultural sector.

International collaborations in agro-terrorism prevention are also bolstered by public awareness efforts. By sharing information and best practices with international partners, law enforcement can create a global network that strengthens our collective defense against agro-terrorism. Public awareness campaigns contribute to this collaboration by fostering a shared understanding of the threats and fostering a sense of collective responsibility.

In conclusion, public awareness is crucial in protecting America's harvest from the threat of agro-terrorism. By educating the public on agro-terrorism threats, promoting active participation, and fostering collaborations, law enforcement can enhance the effectiveness of agricultural biosecurity measures, secure the food supply chain, and ensure the resilience of our agricultural infrastructure. Through research and development of advanced detection methods and public awareness campaigns, we can work together to safeguard our nation's most critical assets – our agricultural resources.

Communicating the Risks of Agro-Terrorism

In today's ever-changing world, the threat of agro-terrorism looms large, posing a significant risk to our nation's agricultural sector, food supply chain, and overall security. As law enforcement professionals entrusted with the safety and well-being of our nation, it is crucial that we understand and effectively communicate the risks associated with agro-terrorism to protect America's harvest.

Agro-terrorism refers to the deliberate introduction of harmful substances or pathogens into the agricultural system, targeting crops, livestock, or food production infrastructure. The consequences of such attacks can be catastrophic, leading to economic losses, public health crises, and widespread panic. Therefore, it is imperative that law enforcement agencies collaborate with agricultural stakeholders, government organizations, and the public to mitigate these risks.

One of the key factors in addressing the threat of agro-terrorism is to raise awareness among the public and those involved in agricultural biosecurity measures. By developing targeted communication strategies, we can ensure that the stakeholders are well-informed about the potential risks, signs of suspicious activities, and appropriate response protocols. Educating farmers, agribusinesses, and agricultural workers about crop protection technologies and strategies is essential in preventing and mitigating agro-terrorism incidents.

Surveillance and monitoring systems play a vital role in detecting and preventing agro-terrorism acts. By implementing advanced technologies such as drones, satellite imagery, and sensors, law enforcement agencies can enhance their capabilities to monitor agricultural facilities, identify potential threats, and initiate prompt responses. This subchapter will delve into the various surveillance and monitoring systems available and how they can be effectively utilized in agro-terrorism prevention.

Furthermore, emergency response protocols must be in place to effectively handle agro-terrorism incidents. Law enforcement agencies should collaborate with first responders, public health officials, and agricultural experts to develop comprehensive response plans. This subchapter will explore the necessary steps to be taken during an agro-terrorism incident, including containment measures, evacuation procedures, and coordination with federal agencies.

An essential aspect of agro-terrorism prevention is conducting risk assessments and developing management strategies. By analyzing vulnerabilities in agricultural infrastructure, supply chains, and critical facilities, law enforcement agencies can prioritize their resources and implement targeted security measures. This subchapter will offer insights into risk assessment methodologies, best practices, and effective management strategies to safeguard our agricultural sector.

International collaborations and partnerships are crucial in combating agro-terrorism. This subchapter will explore existing initiatives and the importance of sharing intelligence, coordinating response efforts, and conducting joint exercises with our international counterparts to strengthen global agro-terrorism prevention.

Public awareness and education campaigns play a crucial role in enhancing the resilience of our agricultural sector. By educating the public about the threats of agro-terrorism, promoting vigilance, and encouraging reporting of suspicious activities, we can create a collective defense against this menace. This subchapter will explore the various communication strategies and public outreach initiatives that law enforcement can adopt to raise awareness.

Finally, research and development of advanced detection methods are essential in staying ahead of agro-terrorism threats. This subchapter will delve into innovative technologies and scientific advancements aimed at enhancing early detection and response capabilities.

By effectively communicating the risks associated with agro-terrorism, law enforcement agencies can galvanize public support, enhance collaboration with stakeholders, and develop proactive strategies to safeguard America's harvest. Together, we can ensure the security and resilience of our agricultural sector, protecting our nation's food supply and the well-being of our citizens.

Public Engagement in Reporting Suspicious

Public Engagement in Reporting Suspicious Activities: A Key Tool in Agro-Terrorism Prevention

One of the most critical aspects of combating agro-terrorism is the active involvement of the public in reporting suspicious activities. Law enforcement agencies play a crucial role in ensuring the protection of the U.S. against agro-terrorism, but they cannot do it alone. By engaging the public, law enforcement can harness the power of collective vigilance and create a strong defense against potential threats to our agricultural sector.

Public engagement in reporting suspicious activities serves as an early warning system, allowing law enforcement to detect and prevent potential agro-terrorism incidents before they occur. The eyes and ears of the public are invaluable in identifying unusual behavior, suspicious purchases, or any other activity that may raise concerns about the safety and security of our food supply chain.

To foster public engagement, law enforcement agencies must prioritize the education and awareness of agro-terrorism threats among the general population. Public awareness campaigns, community outreach programs, and educational initiatives can equip individuals with the knowledge and tools necessary to identify and report suspicious activities effectively.

Furthermore, establishing clear communication channels between law enforcement and the public is essential. This can be achieved through the creation of dedicated hotlines, email addresses, or online platforms where individuals can report any suspicious behavior or activities they come across. Law enforcement agencies should provide clear instructions on what constitutes a suspicious activity and how to report it, ensuring that the public feels empowered and confident in their ability to contribute to the security of our agricultural infrastructure.

Collaboration with agricultural stakeholders is also crucial in engaging the public effectively. By partnering with farmers, agricultural organizations, and industry associations, law enforcement can tap into their expertise and networks to disseminate information and encourage reporting of suspicious activities within the agricultural community. This collaboration ensures that the knowledge and resources necessary for effective reporting are widely accessible among those who are most likely to encounter agro-terrorism threats firsthand.

In conclusion, public engagement in reporting suspicious activities is a vital tool in agro-terrorism prevention. Law enforcement agencies must actively involve the public, raise awareness, and provide clear reporting channels to harness the power of collective vigilance. By engaging the public, law enforcement can establish a robust defense against agro-terrorism, safeguarding our food supply chain, and protecting the integrity of our agricultural sector.